Endorsements

"As someone who has written books, I know what it takes to write a story that would appeal to anyone interested in a better and happier life. Mike has accomplished this and more with *Keep Chopping Wood*. It is a must-read, and I look forward to sharing Mike's exceptional life story with my listeners and readers."—Dave Ramsey, *New York Times* best-selling author and talk radio show host

"Success leaves clues. If you study the lives of successful people, you will find that *who* they are is just as important as *what* they do. Success isn't about luck—it's about determination. It's about putting one foot in front of the other no matter what happens. It's no accident that you are holding this book in your hands right now. As the old saying goes, "When the student is ready, the teacher will appear." Allow Mike Hardwick and his hard-won wisdom to inspire you to reach new heights in every aspect of your life. *Keep Chopping Wood* is the *Think and Grow Rich* of the twenty-first century."—Brad Thor, #1 *New York Times* bestselling author of *Code of Conduct*

"Mike and I have forged a friendship over the past few years and have shared some great conversations about our similar experiences with success and failure. I've always been impressed how Mike has taken his failures and used them as fuel in his internal engine like rocket fuel in pursuit of happiness and the American dream. *Keep Chopping Wood* is a book that I relate to personally and have found to be an inspiration as I continue to work hard and experience various degrees of success and failure. I would recommend this book to anyone who has a passion for hard work and entrepreneurism, and never puts down the hammer or the axe. Just keep on *Chopping Wood* and you'll get there!"—John Rich, singer and songwriter with the music group Big and Rich

"I've known Mike most of my life and have been constantly amazed and impressed with his business acumen and his generous heart. In this captivating book, Mike has shared many of his secrets to success as well as the challenges that invariably come from being at the top of one's game. I know readers will learn so much from his remarkable life, and enjoy his journey as one of the most respected business leaders in the country."—Former U.S. Congressman Bob Clement (D-TN)

"Every entrepreneur, business owner, and parent should read this book. Mike Hardwick tells his life story—from a truly humble beginning to successful entrepreneur. He shares the lessons he learned along the way both as a boy and as a man—his failures and disappointments, and his joys and successes. He shares his personal philosophy of service, learning, winning, and losing. I finished his book with lots of new ideas and was energized and inspired. Read this book!"—Tom Black, author, sales and marketing coach, and entrepreneur

"I was deeply moved and encouraged by reading Mike Hardwick's inspirational account of his life. We never know what a person has had to endure to achieve financial and spiritual success. Nothing is ever as easy as it appears. This important book should be required reading for teenagers and would-be entrepreneurs. Mike's story drives home the point that success is not achieved overnight and that the wisdom gleaned from godly parents has a lasting impact."—Carol M. Swain, PhD, professor of political science and professor of law, Vanderbilt University

"Mike and I have known each other for several years now. He and his family were our neighbors during my years in Nashville as the defensive coordinator of the Tennessee Titans. We treasure our friendship with the Hardwick family. We have stayed in contact through my years as the head coach of the Detroit Lions and defensive coordinator of the Buffalo Bills and Philadelphia Eagles. Mike has entertained us with his many thoughts on football, and even though he is a lifelong Green Bay Packers fan, his stories are priceless. In his new book, *Keep Chopping Wood*, Mike weaves both humor and real life stories into life-changing ideas. Readers will learn many highly valuable secrets of living a life with thoughtful purpose each and every day!"—Jim Schwartz, NFL defensive coordinator for the Philadelphia Eagles

"A very thought-provoking and compelling read. The introspection is courageous, and many life lessons can be learned or recaptured. It's applicable to all walks of life."—Dan Crockett, president/CEO, Franklin American Mortgage Company

"Mike Hardwick is a special leader who has a unique gift to see the best and bring out the best in everyone he touches. I've had the privilege and gift to benefit from Mike's valuable life lessons and stories for years. This book is a treasure chest of stories and keys to success that I can't wait to share with my employees, clients, and even my kids."—Dave Savage, founder/owner of Mortgage Coach

"Mike Hardwick's story should be required reading for every entrepreneur. After enduring a catastrophic business failure, Mike learns what really matters in life—faith, family, and friendships. His journey led him to live his life by following his 'daily disciplines.' Although all of them are great things to live by, my personal favorite is to 'connect with family.' As simple as that sounds, I have known many entrepreneurs who have lost connection with their families during the process of building a company. Too many ended in divorce, and many of those that did not, never had the connectedness with family that leads to rich and lasting relationships. I am thankful every day that I learned this lesson in my life before it was too late. What truly matters in life is not the size of the business we build or the wealth it creates. I would much rather have a life that is full of wonderful memories of times with my children and grandchildren than feeling alone with piles of money and stuff that I really never have time to enjoy. As the old George Strait song reminds us, 'I ain't never seen a hearse with a luggage rack.' Thanks to Mike for offering such an honest and personal story that reminds us of what a life well-lived really can look like."—Dr. Jeff Cornwall, professor and Jack C. Massey Chair of Entrepreneurship, Belmont University

"I've had the pleasure of traveling, vacationing, and working with Mike for over twenty years. Mike used to tell me, "People change. But not much." Thankfully, that's true of Mike. He's the same generous, values-centered man today as he was twenty years ago. One of my favorite joys in life is to hear Mike Hardwick tell a story. *Keep Chopping Wood* is full of wonderful stories packed with life and business lessons. The writing is so friendly and conversational it's hard to put the book down. I can't wait for the audio version!"—Dean Jackson, international sales and marketing guru

"Mike Hardwick knows leadership! *Keep Chopping Wood* is a thoroughly engaging read that masterfully teaches endearing principles on leadership and life. You will be captivated by his wisdom and will be blessed by his knowledge."—Todd Duncan, *New York Times* best-selling author

"In his book, *Keep Chopping Wood*, Mike not only does a masterful job at honoring the true mentors in his life, weaving together countless personal and entertaining stories, but also extracts them into a manuscript of lessons for better living. A model that is as genuine as it is powerful. I have witnessed firsthand its impact on my life and on so many others. I encourage not only a businessperson to read this book, but anyone who truly desires to learn from the experiences of others and evolve toward a life of true legacy and persistent giving, like Mike has for so many years."—Matthew C. Clarke, chief operating officer and CFO of Churchill Mortgage Corporation

"Mike is one of those rare people you meet in life who has managed to live by the words and deeds he espouses. His book *Keep Chopping Wood* not only gives anyone who reads it hope and faith for the future, but also shows how living a life in service to others and God can make all of the difference. I am confident that anyone who reads this wonderful book will appreciate Mike's generosity of heart and spirit and the willingness to share his life story in such a personal and thought-provoking way."—Cecil Kemp, CPA and business entrepreneur

"Mike is so blessed to have the parents he has had and how they loved him and taught him; that is so amazing. Mike wrote a beautiful story in his book *Keep Chopping Wood* about how he learned to take all the goodness that was given to him and make something extraordinary out of that experience. What comes to mind is the parable of the talents (Matthew 25:14–30; Luke 19:12–28) that says, 'You have been faithful in a few things'; I would put him in charge of many things."—Joe Stumpf, marketing guru and founder/owner of By Referral Only

"When God distributed personality, generosity and enthusiasm, I believe Mike Hardwick received a double dose! His most appealing book no doubt will serve its readers as inspiration, entertainment, and encouragement as he shares both temporary failures and heartaches coupled with substantial tangible and intangible achievements. *Keep Chopping Wood* provides many examples for us all to contemplate and appreciate as we continue through our lives that God has provided us; many thanks!" —George H. Armistead III, CEO, Answers by Armistead LLC

"*Keep Chopping Wood* is a fascinating look into the heart and mind of one of America's great success stories—my friend Mike Hardwick. I treasure the opportunities to talk to and learn from Mike, and I am thrilled that he decided to memorialize his most critical life lessons and business principles through this book. I encourage anyone who is interested in how to be successful in the business world and, most importantly, successful with family and with life, to take advantage of the opportunity to learn from one of the best. Thank you, Mike, for sharing your heart and your life with me through your friendship, and for sharing with me and the world through *Keep Chopping Wood*. I am encouraged and inspired by your words. I couldn't put it down once I started reading, and I have already referred back to the wisdom you share as I consider how to order my life and my professional career."—Barry Booker, banker and basketball sports commentator on the SEC Network

"Through the story of his life, Mike has embedded lessons on leadership, management, and personal development. As a friend and business associate, I've traveled, lived, worked, laughed, and cried with Mike for two decades, and I can tell you from firsthand experience his commitment to the principles he shares has been consistent. How he makes people feel, maximizes their skills and talents, instills a sense of mission, and develops each team member is the secret sauce of Churchill Mortgage. Mike talks a lot about his own mentors, and I count him as one of my top five mentors in life. Much of what I've learned is in the pages of *Keep Chopping Wood*."—Jim McQuaig, top mortgage industry producer, and business partner of Mike Hardwick for over two decades

"Mike Hardwick and I have only known each other a few years, but we've known each other all our lives. How is that possible? We are about the same age, both grew up in Tennessee, both sons of hard-working families with deep convictions about religion, the value of hard work, the commitment to treat others as you want to be treated, and the importance of commitment to family. Our dads were both products of the Depression, and both were marked for life by those events. Mike and I both suffered losses from the Tax Reform Act of 1986, but both of us decided to be better, not bitter. And now Mike has written a masterpiece in his new book, *Keep Chopping Wood*. It's a story that every young man or woman should read, and then reread. There are some people that you meet, and you instantly know that you were just meant to know them. That's Mike and me. I'm honored to call him my friend, and I'm honored to recommend his book."—Turney Stevens, dean emeritus and director, Dean Institute for Corporate Governance and Integrity, Lipscomb University

"When I first met Mike Hardwick I immediately sensed his presence. It was one of quiet calm confidence and peace. It was radiating. I was attracted to his experience, depth, and sincere appreciation for life and growth. I knew he was someone I wanted to work with. I then began to coach and develop the talent at Churchill and can see now after reading *Keep Chopping Wood* how the culture has become so strong and centered on values and principles. This book shows you, the entrepreneur, how one's past scripting and influence shapes a person for their bigger future. It shows you how to bounce back and fight through failure. I found myself captivated by Mike's early influences and how his vision manifested into reality by leveraging his unique past into building something very special. It's unique and different in a world of sameness and commodity. I urge you to read this book and open up your dreamer just like Mike did and use it to find your ingredients for success."—coach Micheal Burt, Ten time author, former championship coach, business growth expert

Mike Hardwick
with Dava Guerin

KEEP CHOPPING WOOD

A Pastor's Son Who Had
it All, Lost it All, and then
Regained True Wealth

Foreword by Dave Ramsey

WESTBOW
PRESS®
A DIVISION OF THOMAS NELSON
& ZONDERVAN

Cover/Author Photo by Russ Harrington
Interior shots supplied by Mike Hardwick and other shots by Russ Harrington
Photos of Megan and Mish's wedding, Clark Brewer Photography
*Russ Harrington shots are numbers, 36, 37, 46, 49b, 76
*Brent Harrington numbers are, 23, 32, 31, 64, 68

This book is a work of non-fiction. Unless otherwise noted, the author and the publisher make no explicit guarantees as to the accuracy of the information contained in this book and in some cases, names of people and places have been altered to protect their privacy.

Scripture taken from the Holy Bible, NEW INTERNATIONAL VERSION®. Copyright © 1973, 1978, 1984, 2011 by Biblica, Inc. All rights reserved worldwide. Used by permission. NEW INTERNATIONAL VERSION® and NIV® are registered trademarks of Biblica, Inc. Use of either trademark for the offering of goods or services requires the prior written consent of Biblica US, Inc.

WestBow Press books may be ordered through booksellers or by contacting:

WestBow Press
A Division of Thomas Nelson & Zondervan
1663 Liberty Drive
Bloomington, IN 47403
www.westbowpress.com
1 (866) 928-1240

Because of the dynamic nature of the Internet, any web addresses or links contained in this book may have changed since publication and may no longer be valid. The views expressed in this work are solely those of the author and do not necessarily reflect the views of the publisher, and the publisher hereby disclaims any responsibility for them.

Any people depicted in stock imagery provided by Thinkstock are models, and such images are being used for illustrative purposes only.
Certain stock imagery © Thinkstock.

ISBN: 978-1-5127-4898-7 (sc)
ISBN: 978-1-5127-4897-0 (hc)
ISBN: 978-1-5127-4896-3 (e)

Library of Congress Control Number: 2016911059

Print information available on the last page.

WestBow Press rev. date: 9/14/2016

Dedication

This book is dedicated to my sweet, loving, and beautiful wife, Stephanie, whose infectious smile and incredible energy amaze me. You have allowed me much freedom to spend countless hours working on this project, time that I usually would have spent with you. There is no way for me to really measure or adequately express how much I love and appreciate you. Your love and support mean the world to me, as you are truly my best friend. Also my four talented and loving children, Shayna, Megan, Lawson, and Michael, who are the pride of my life, and are a wonderful reflection of all the best their parents have to offer. You all have made our lives immeasurably more meaningful and amazing. I deeply appreciate my devoted and inspirational parents, Rev. L. H. Hardwick Jr. and Montelle Hardwick, and my brother, Steve, who made my boyhood years such fulfilling ones. Lastly, my ever-present grandparents, Pop and Maggie Carson, and Pop and Grandmother Hardwick. They were such devoted and loving family, whose memories will forever shower those they touched with the greatest gifts of all—faith, love, and compassion. I simply cannot imagine ever having been blessed with a more incredible and wonderful family!

Contents

Foreword

It is no understatement to say that Mike Hardwick played an instrumental role in changing my life. We met as kids in Nashville, Tennessee, both sharing a love of sports, finance, marketing, and belief in the power and glory of God. We worked for years in the real estate and banking industries, Mike helping grow a condominium conversion company into one of the most successful in the United States during the 1980s, and me a profitable $4 million real estate portfolio at the tender age of twenty-six. Then, when the financial crisis hit in 1986 as a result of the Tax Reform Act, we both hit rock bottom at the same time, watching our wealth and success take an unexpected 180-degree turn, unsure what our futures would hold.

I will never forget that day when we were both sitting at a local restaurant lamenting our situations when I approached Mike with the idea of me starting a new talk radio show with a struggling radio station. I was hoping to use it as a template for starting my own radio show focusing on helping people to not make the same mistakes I did in terms of money management and personal finance. While Mike at first wasn't keen on the idea, wondering how I could make money doing a talk radio show on a bankrupt station no one listened to, soon after I made the deal and started my own broadcast, Mike became my first and largest advertiser. He still is advertising on my show to this day!

In Mike's new book, *Keep Chopping Wood: A Pastor's Son Who Had It All, Lost It All and Then Regained True Wealth*, he not only gives readers the inside story of his remarkable life, but also an in-depth look into the world of business—including how to build a corporate culture based on excellence, compassion, and giving, motivating employees to be good stewards of the blessings they have been given, successfully incorporating family members into a business, and planning and executing a philanthropy strategy for the long-term. He shares with readers growing up with a father who was also the pastor of one of the fastest-growing and largest churches in the nation, and parents and grandparents who taught him and his brother the value of money and hard work at a very young age. He courageously shares his bout with depression, his philosophy for living a happy and productive life, and stories about Mike's sports and business heroes that will surely inspire anyone who reads this wonderful book.

As someone who has written numerous *New York Times* best-selling books, I know what it takes to write a story that would appeal to anyone interested in a better and happier life. Mike has accomplished this and more with *Keep Chopping Wood*. It is a must-read, and I look forward to sharing Mike's exceptional life story with my listeners and readers.

Dave Ramsey, January 2016

Acknowledgments

There are so many people I want to thank for giving me the inspiration and encouragement to put my life's experiences in a book like this. It has been a labor of love and a wonderful project in which to be involved. I can say without reservation that I have always strived to reach just a little further in each area of my life, and writing a book was certainly a stretch for me! It has been said that when you thoroughly exhaust an experience, then you don't have to look back with any regret. I am so very thankful for the opportunity to write this book.

First and foremost I want to thank God, for without His love, mercy, and direction I would not be where I am today. This project would have never come to life without the help and guidance of Dava Guerin, a gifted writer who helped me tell my life story in an interesting and compelling manner. Dava, you kept me focused and forging forward on this wonderful project. You have been a true pleasure to work with! Matt Clarke was instrumental in gathering historical material from our company archives, and arranging interviews and meetings with many of our key employees. My son, Lawson, and daughters, Megan and Shayna, provided their invaluable insights into our company as well as we moved the project along over the past year. Our long-term employees, many of whom have been with me from the early days of Churchill Mortgage, which I founded more than twenty-four years ago, shared many of their stories and experiences since they started at Churchill Mortgage. They include: Marisa Shapter, Stephanie Christian, Doug Walker, Kathy Cook, Gina Adams, Jim McQuaig, and Josh Phillips, among so many others. My aunt, Mary (Witsie) Clement and her husband, former US Congressman Bob Clement (D-TN), introduced me to Dava, and they have both helped me understand the writing process and the value of capturing your life for eternity on paper. My good friend, Dave Ramsey, was one of the first people I shared the book with, and his insights and suggestions helped me think through just what was important in a memoir and what folks would enjoy reading. For that I am grateful. My sister-in-law, Debbie Burson, who went back to college after having reared four beautiful daughters and earned her doctorate degree in education, and who helped review the book and offered solid insight. Debbie, you have earned my deep respect. Two amazing and wonderful friends, Dr. James L. Fortner and Cecil Kemp, who helped me in so many ways with sound counsel and advice over the years, especially during Churchill Mortgage's infancy. Finally, my mentor, Dick Freeman, who helped instill in me the emotional foundation and business experience that to this day I continue to call upon for advice and inspiration.

Introduction

Putting our pens to paper on that warm, sunny day in July was exhilarating. After many, many meetings with our negotiating teams of lawyers and accountants in downtown Nashville, Tennessee, finally we were blessed to be able to sign the last documents that would change the lives of most of my business partners and many of our shareholders forever. Many of these very happy investors were just about to become millionaires, many times over.

There were originally eight of us, and each took a risk fourteen years before by personally investing nearly $5 million of the $6 million capital we needed to start a bank in the heart of Music City. It was called Franklin National Bank and it grew into one of the most successful and profitable community banks in the country. Why? Because along with my good friend, Gordon Inman, who was our CEO and chairman, and the other six founders, we wanted to try an innovative approach to banking at the time—truly putting the customer first, being conservative with our investments, investing heavily in our local real estate economy, and creating new products and services that we knew from our extensive research would appeal to the marketplace at the time. And it worked.

From our opening day on December 1, 1989, to just fourteen years later, we successfully grew Franklin National Bank to approximately $1 billion in total assets. Then, on June 10, 2004, we sold the bank to Fifth Third Bank out of Cincinnati, Ohio, for arguably one of the highest multiples of any community bank ever sold in the country up to that time.

After initially serving as executive vice president of Franklin National Bank and being very involved in the daily tasks of starting and building a federally chartered bank for the initial three years, I resigned from the bank while retaining my stock and staying on as a board member, and then decided to start another new venture.

On March 13, 1992, I decided to put my knowledge and experience in the banking industry where I had been involved in various capacities to the test. Having built a condominium conversion company from scratch, thanks to the help and confidence of my mentor Dick Freeman, and building it into one of the largest companies of its kind in the 1980s, I wanted to use that foundation, as well as the success of Franklin National Bank, to build a business of my own. I was forty years old at the time and knew I could start another venture that would not only make money, but also help Americans achieve their dream of homeownership. While I didn't have any visions of grandeur, I still had a burning desire to build something on my own.

But it hasn't always been easy. In fact, after having such a high degree of success very early in my business career with the condo conversion company, I thought that I was figuratively on top of the world. I was making an annual income of mid-six figures, and I must admit back then I might have even been a bit too self-centered and overconfident. Then, suddenly, my world came crashing down around me. It was October 22, 1986, and President Reagan signed the Tax Reform Act, which essentially reformed the major internal revenue laws of the United States. It was introduced in the US House of Representatives by Dan Rostenkowski (D-IL), and was designed to simplify the tax code and achieve revenue neutrality by decreasing individual income taxes, eliminating $30 billion annually in loopholes, and increasing corporate and capital gains taxes. But with that one simple stroke of the pen, and the bill's signature by the president making it the new law of the land, my entire business operation came to a standstill.

Why did this happen? Ironically, what the law was intended to remedy in actuality drove countless companies out of business, put so many people out of work, and reduced the primary home lenders to a shadow of their former selves. That was due to the fact that the law was also made retroactive so that all of the investments in real estate made under the former laws, which allowed legal write-offs of losses and other expenses, were substantially taken away. Now the value of those investments made under the previous laws was irreparably damaged. Not only did the law force our company into total bankruptcy, but I personally lost almost everything; I felt like a total failure. I felt that I had completely let my family down and didn't know how I would ever be able to come back financially. I had *failed* at something for the first time in my entire life. I was devastated financially and emotionally, and the horrifying experience triggered a clinical depression that lasted for approximately one year. Through the love of my parents, family, and friends, and my rediscovered faith, I was able to overcome my feelings of despair and hopelessness and rebuild my life both internally and externally.

Once I got back on my feet again, I knew I wanted to start a new venture of my own using what I learned from my business success and failure and do it completely on my terms. On March 13, 1992, I founded Churchill Mortgage Corporation, the name inspired by one of my heroes—Winston Churchill. He was one of the greatest leaders of the twentieth century, and without him, the world might have been under the control of Hitler and his genocidal Nazi cohorts. Thankfully, Churchill would never give up, wouldn't relent in his desire to eradicate evil, and motivated Britain and its allies to withstand and conquer the Nazi menace. In tribute to his tenacity, motivation, persistence, and drive, I wanted to memorialize those attributes when I named my business and create a corporate culture that embraced those values and more.

Unlike other mortgage companies I researched or was involved in, I wanted Churchill Mortgage to be something more. I knew it would take a lot of work, great devotion, and perseverance to build anything of significance. But I was willing to put in the hard work. As another great writer and thought leader of my generation, the leadership guru and best-selling author John Maxwell says in his analogy of the law of the flywheel: "Once you build the big wheel windmill and actually get it moving, it eventually takes less and less energy to keep it going."

For me, my big wheel would be comprised of these lofty but attainable business core values: putting people over profits; highly valuing employees and treating them right; showing genuine respect and honor for others; making the dream of homeownership affordable for everyone; achieving a work/life balance; and fostering the qualities of trustworthiness, excellence, philanthropy, positive attitude, and humility, through ongoing education and mentorship. Twenty-three years later, I'm proud to say that we have achieved those goals and much more. Churchill Mortgage annually closes well in excess of $1 billion in residential home loans, and is recognized nationwide as one of the most profitable and respected independent mortgage companies in the United States.

All of this could never have been accomplished without having a solid foundation. Not just in the bricks and mortar sense but those invaluable building blocks to achieve a happy, fulfilling and successful life: a stable home, loving and involved parents and grandparents, and teachers and mentors that support you along the way. For me, my dad and mom, as well as both sets of grandparents, gave me that solid footing to help me fulfill my dreams and passions. I learned the art of salesmanship because my parents enlisted me and my brother to sell Krispy Kreme doughnuts and hot cooked meals door-to-door to the small businesses and individual homeowners in our hometown when I was a young boy.

I learned to value all human beings and treat them with respect from my parents, as well as the value of hard work. While the road wasn't always easy, it was the one that led me home. As Dad once told me, "Son, it's not about looking at how many times you fall down, but how many times you are going to get back up!" And that echoes what the author Austin O'Malley once said: "The fact that you have been knocked down is interesting, but the length of time you remain down is important." In life, all of us will have problems. Rather than wallowing in defeat, I am convinced that getting back on our feet is the best medicine.

Dad was the founder and pastor of Christ Church, Nashville, Tennessee, one of the largest and most impactful megachurches in the South. Dad and my grandfather Hardwick, together with a few men in the church in those very early days, literally built their first church building with their own hands. Dad was a very young man, in his early twenties, when he led this small band of dedicated men to accomplish a task that seemed unfathomable at the time.

The lessons Dad, Mom, and my grandparents taught me about business and life were invaluable. They provided the foundation for my business success, as well as how to overcome life's challenges and disappointments which all of us inevitably face during our lifetime. One of my chief goals for this book is to share those ideas and lessons with my family, employees, customers, and anyone else who wants to dream big and have those dreams make a difference.

Life is a journey, and it all begins at home.

CHAPTER 1

The Value of a Solid Foundation: From Doughnuts to Million-Dollar Mortgages

> We leave something of ourselves behind when we leave a place; we stay there, even though we go away. And there are things in us that we can find again only by going back there.—Pascal Mercier, *Night Train to Lisbon*

When I was a young boy, around the age of eight, we lived in a small two-bedroom, one-bath house on Sadler Street on the outskirts of Nashville, Tennessee. It was in the late 1950s, a simpler time where the world was in a relatively peaceful state and our main concerns were hitting a baseball, riding our bikes, and playing with our buddies at the Coleman Park Community Center near our home. My younger brother, Steve, and I were the best of friends, and folks in our small town knew us very, very well. Not because we got into trouble or called too much attention to ourselves. No, we were the preacher's sons, and every Saturday for as long as I could remember, we made the lives of many of the local business owners on Nolensville Road just a little bit sweeter. Who knew that fifty-plus years later I would be chairman and CEO of my own company, and help so many Americans achieve their goal of homeownership?

Rev. Lawson H. Hardwick Jr., my dad, I guess you could say is simply a force of nature. His sparkling green-blue eyes and gentle broad smile attract people to him like flies to flypaper. It's been that way all of his life. Ever since I could remember, he knew the value of hard work. After all, when he was just eighteen years old and already a husband and soon-to-be father, Dad wanted to become a pastor and serve the people around him no matter what their lot in life or status in the community. He was truly a man of the people and is the kindest, most loving person I have ever known.

Dad's dream was to build a church for the glory of God. He was only eighteen years old when he married a beautiful nineteen-year-old girl by the name of Montelle, and despite his youth, had the drive and determination to start a church. I have often asked my father what made him think that he could accomplish that feat and actually convince folks to bring their families to a church led by an eighteen-year-old man. He told me that he felt a keen "calling" and actually never considered doing anything else. That same inspiration and calling was apparent to him even when he was just a lad of twelve.

While he was working a full-time job, and also attending Freewill Baptist Bible College, located on the west side of Nashville, he worked day and night to pastor a start-up church. But in those early years of his ministry, the small fledging church Dad was working so hard to grow simply didn't have enough members to provide an income for our family to live. Dad had a string of full-time jobs to support our little family, which by that time included my mom, Montelle; my brother, Steve; and, of course, me. Dad sold vacuum cleaners and cemetery plots, served as the chaplain of the Tennessee State Prison for seven years, and even drove a Colonial Bread truck route, anything to keep a roof over our heads and food in our mouths. Dad knew the value of hard work, persistence, and perseverance.

With very little money, yet a strong desire to build a bricks and mortar church, Dad decided to take matters into his own hands and start the construction process on a wing and a prayer. Fortunately, he came from a long line of homebuilders, so he knew how to design and erect a structure that could hold at least a small congregation comfortably. It was nothing fancy, for sure, but Dad was determined to get the job done.

He was very persistent in his vision of his "calling" and never wavered from doing whatever it took to fulfill that calling.

Lesson Number One: Keep Chopping Wood.

Every morning around 5:00 AM, Dad would wake up, have a cup of coffee and a small breakfast of toast and eggs, and then get to work selling his vacuum cleaners or cemetery plots, only to return home and begin work on his church construction project. With the help of other men in his fledgling new church, and a good dose of sweat equity, in about eighteen to twenty months the basement church was built on a small parcel of land on Elberta Street in Woodbine, a small community on the outskirts of South Nashville. He named it Woodbine Pentecostal Church, and I can still remember how large it looked to me as a child, yet in reality it was only about twelve hundred to fifteen hundred square feet. The pews were small and made out of oak. I remember the small sanctuary, which had poles right in the middle of the space. The altar was very plain and simple; the floors were made of tile, and the roof was flat, yet when you were in that little basement building, you could feel the overwhelming presence of God in every oak panel pew and smooth sanded altar. Since Dad and the other men of the church had to work full-time jobs on weekdays, they could only work on building our church during the late afternoon and on Saturdays, so it took longer than usual to complete. Dad was so proud of that little church once it was finally built. We were proud of him, too.

Lesson Number Two: Great Things Take Time.

I guess one might say that having a solid foundation in life helps jump-start a person's path to happiness and success. If that is the case, then Dad not only did that for Steve and me in the figurative sense, but also quite literally. I would say that Woodbine Pentecostal Church became the symbol to me of rock solid faith, honesty, integrity, and, most importantly, truly loving and treating other people with dignity and respect.

Though at the time we probably had only about one hundred parishioners, Dad had their full support, and they knew he loved and cared about them. Dad and Mom would work eight hours a day during the week on their public jobs, come home to quickly feed and care for Steve and me, and then we would all go to visit the church families in their homes. Dad and Mom were doing the work of the Lord, and they taught us boys the importance of really caring for others. Dad felt that being a good pastor meant you were there for people during the important times in their lives such as births, sicknesses, marriages, baby dedications, funerals, and any other time of great human need. People would often say to me, "Mike, someday you will follow in your father's footsteps." They were sure big shoes to fill.

During those first twenty or so years, our little church was beginning to build a name for itself, and Dad was gaining a reputation for being a man of the people, a person to look up to and come to in times of trouble. He was able to harness his superior sales ability and boundless energy to not only attract new members to the church but also raise money to keep the lights on. Back then, he never took a salary, either. Not one dime! He was fortunate that his endless energy, charm, and youth enabled him to work two jobs, pastor in the evenings and on the weekends, and concoct creative ways to fund-raise to keep our little church financially afloat. Dad and Mom were always the first to arrive and the last to leave. They really did lead by example.

Lesson Number Three: Actions Speak Louder than Words.

Dad believed that his two sons should learn the value of hard work and discipline, and once we were old enough to fully comprehend those lessons, he put his theory to the test.

It was a dark, cool summer morning, and I was about nine or ten years old when I learned two very important lessons: how to sell, and the value of hard work.

"Boys, get up; I know it's Saturday, but we need to get going," Dad said.

"But, Dad, I'm tired. Can I sleep a little longer?" I said, as I wiped the sleep from my eyes.

"Come on, Son; I'm serious. Remember what I told you last week, that if you work with your brother and you both do a good job today, you'll get a special reward." Dad always knew just what to say. He sure had a way with words.

So we boys rolled out of bed, brushed our teeth, and washed our faces, and got dressed in a hurry, and Dad and Mom packed us into our Oldsmobile station wagon—an iconic symbol of America in the 1950s—and off we drove to the church. By then it was about 6:00 AM, and Steve and I were barely awake as the early morning sun began to pierce the darkness. Dad was, of course, raring to go. We dropped Mom off at the church on Elberta Street, where she joined about six to eight other women who were already getting the kitchen prepared for cooking lunch, and we headed off to a new business location in downtown Nashville.

Dad drove our old Oldsmobile with us boys lying in the back seat, still a bit sleepy and fast falling back to sleep, to downtown Nashville on Lafayette Street. When we arrived, he anxiously said, "Boys, wake up. We have work to do!" We jumped out of the car and ran in to enjoy the enticing smell of sweet, freshly baked Krispy Kreme doughnuts. I can still vividly remember how much I wanted to eat those heavenly treats, but Dad had another plan for Steve and me.

Lesson Number Four: Work First, and Then Play!

The reason we were on this mission in the first place was to raise money for the church, and as I would later find out, also teach my brother and me the invaluable lesson of the importance of hard work and perseverance.

"Dad, can you tell us what we are doing again?" I asked as I begged him to let me eat a freshly baked doughnut.

"Son, we're going to the doughnut shop to buy a few hundred dozen hot doughnuts, then you and Steve will sell them for seventy cents for one dozen or two for a dollar, depending on what the customer wants. Remember what I told you boys; this will help us raise money for the church and also help you and Steve get to know our neighbors. Beside the point, learning how to sell is a skill you can really use as you get older," Dad said.

"Okay, Dad, but can Steve and I have an extra doughnut if we do a good job?" Dad just smiled. Even though I knew he would give me that extra Krispy Kreme, I also knew he meant business. Dad wanted us to learn the value of hard work and the importance of being productive.

As we pulled into the driveway at Krispy Kreme, Dad picked up the doughnuts in large cardboard boxes. We headed back to the church to meet up with a few of the other men and boys from our church, and then we divided the boxes of doughnuts into equal numbers. Each father and his son were given instructions to head out to the various streets in Woodbine. Of course, Steve and I were raring to go by this point and get down to the business at hand. As Dad drove our old Oldsmobile up and down the streets of Woodbine, he watched us like a hawk as we walked along both sides of the street literally going door to door asking our neighbors if they wanted to buy our sweet delicacies.

My tactic was pretty simple. I was a clean-cut kid, and always dressed in a freshly pressed shirt and nice, clean pressed jeans. Mom and Dad believed in making a good first impression. I practiced what I would say over and over in my mind until it became almost second nature. I must admit I was a little nervous at first, but like anything else in life, practice does really make perfect—well almost!

"Hi, my name is Mike Hardwick, and I'm selling hot doughnuts so that Dad can buy an organ for our church," I said, as I anxiously waited to hear the person's response. "I can give you a good price, Mister, if you want to buy more than one. Would you like to buy two dozen?" Nine times out of ten, the folks would say, "Thank you, son. I'll take two dozen." That was music to my ears. Imagine, me, a nine-year-old boy, making such a sale on my first try. Dad had done a good job telling us boys how to "up sell." It was an exhilarating feeling, and soon I even looked forward to my Saturday mornings on the road with my family.

But hot doughnuts were not my only product offering at the time; meals on wheels were my latest addition to my sales pitch. Here's how it worked: after dropping Mom off at the church, she and all of the church ladies were busy at the church making hot lunches, too. Each week they would vary the menus. One day they would cook meat loaf, mashed potatoes, and collard greens, and the next week they would prepare roasted chicken with green beans, sweet tea, and sometimes even lemon pie.

Lesson Number Five: There Can Be No Success Without the Equal Support of a Loving Family.

After we finished selling all the doughnuts, we would then meet back at the church for our next task of the day. The men and boys would learn what the ladies were planning for their menu for that day, and then we would head out to begin taking orders for plate lunches from businesspeople in the community. In those days in the 1950s and 1960s, there were all kinds of small locally owned businesses in the Woodbine community. Back then, most small to mid-size businesses were family owned and operated. On Nolensville Pike were clothing stores, hardware stores, small motels, drugstores and everything you would expect in a small town in the South at the time.

I was just a boy, so going into a business to try and sell a plate lunch to a businessman was more than intimidating, to say the least. I vividly remember feeling a bit nervous at first, but soon I felt like a real pro. Dad was a great teacher, and he taught Steve and me the art of salesmanship.

This is how I would approach a potential customer and what I would say to him when I first walked through the door. I would say, "Sir, my mom is the best cook ever, and she is making something special for lunch today. For just $1.50, I can bring you a hot lunch by noon. Everybody loves her cooking, too, and if you buy her lunch plate, we can get enough money to buy a piano for our church. Oh, Mister, I forgot. She can make more than one plate, for the people who work for you, too."

With those compelling words, I was able to sell many, many hot lunches and Krispy Kreme doughnuts. Mom and Dad were proud of my brother and me, and I got tremendous satisfaction from being able to help my family and our church.

Most of all, I learned at a very young age the value of hard work. Of getting up early on a Saturday morning when all I wanted to do was stay in bed. Talking to complete strangers and building relationships with them just by selling hot Krispy Kreme doughnuts and home-cooked lunches. But most of all, I learned how to sell, a crucial skill that helped me create and grow businesses in the financial and real estate industries, which has provided solid jobs for so many good people, and, of course, has helped make many people exceptionally wealthy. But just like building a home, a solid foundation is the key to a productive and fulfilling life, and I was truly blessed to have learned from the master.

Lesson Number Six: No One Is a Stranger When You Treat Them as a Friend.

As I said, Mom had a way about her that was strong and powerful, and at the same time, caring and loving. She was the consummate preacher's wife—always there for the congregation, offering advice and helping anyone who was in pain, suffering, or just wanted someone there to listen. Her parents, my grandparents, were a huge influence in my life, as were Dad's parents. Among the six of them, I was surrounded by people who were different in terms of their professions and backgrounds, but they shared a number of very important qualities such as empathy, compassion, perseverance, and forgiveness.

Growing up, I am certain my brother, Steve, and I tested their values many, many times. Mom and Dad knew when to dole out hefty doses of those qualities in an effort to help us become responsible young men. But like any good parents, they also weren't afraid to use the proverbial rod when necessary.

Now, don't get the impression that Mom and Dad were hurting us in any way; absolutely not. Yes, the proverbial rod did hurt a little, but the lessons I learned from my parents' loving correction were much needed by me in my early years. No doubt I would never have learned how to act responsibly, respect and treat others properly, put important things first before playing, and so much more, without my parents being willing to teach me in this manner when necessary. Their collective goal was to teach us those meaningful life lessons that they wisely knew would give us a solid foundation, and stand the test of time.

Lesson Number Seven: Sparing the Rod Does Spoil the Child.

That's why they were so powerful and memorable. Like the time Mom caught me doing something that we all know as human beings is just plain wrong: Stealing!

I always loved gadgets and taking things apart and putting them back together. For some people, the devil is in the details, but for me, the details were what attracted me to a task or project more than anything else in the world, especially when I was around ten years old.

One of my favorite hobbies at that age was putting together and painting model cars. Every weekend, I would go with Mom to Garrett's Drug Store on Nolensville Road, which was one of my very favorite stores at the time. They had model car kits in colorful boxes complete with a picture of the car, let's say '61 Mercury, and all of the materials to put the car together. Each box included all of the parts to build the small six- by eight-inch car—the chassis, the wheels, and axles, and, of course, the chrome hardware. The only thing it didn't include in the box was paints and brushes. Those we had to buy separately to complete the project.

I was very proud of my model car collection, too, and I would have all of the finished products lined up neatly on my dresser in my bedroom.

One rainy Saturday afternoon in the summer, Mom took me back to Garrett's Drugs to purchase another model car. I was so excited and almost couldn't fall asleep the night before just thinking about buying my next model car. "Son, let's get going; we have to get to Garrett's before it closes, and I know how much you want to get another model car," she said. "Thanks, Mom. I'll be ready in a second."

As we entered the store I said hello to the owner, Mr. Garrett, and Mom and I walked over to the aisle where all of the model cars were neatly displayed. "Mom, can I get this Mercury? I just love it, and I can't wait to put it together," I said, hardly containing my excitement. Of course Mom said, "Yes." Mom paid the bill, and we both left the store for the short trip back home. When we arrived, I ran right to my bedroom and immediately broke into that box and began to work on building that model car. A couple of hours later—imagining in my mind what the shiny car would look like when it was finished, I noticed that all of the parts were not there. To my huge disappointment, the rear axle was missing. I couldn't believe it. What was I going to do? "Hey, everybody, the axle is missing from the box. Can you help me look for it," I said, as I anxiously searched everywhere but to no avail.

Fortunately, Mom was headed back to Garrett's only a few days later, and I asked her if I could tag along. We drove back to the store and greeted Mr. Garrett. Mom walked over to the aisle where the sewing supplies were located, and I headed right back to the aisle where the model cars were. I looked around the store to make sure no one could see me, and slipped quietly over to where I could view a new, unopened model car box, the same kind that Mom bought for me but was missing its axle. Once I could discern that no one was around, I gently removed the tape holding the box together, reached in the box to feel around for the axle, then did what I thought was right. I picked up the part, put it in my pocket and went around to the front of the store to find Mom.

As we were leaving, I touched the small axle in my right pants pocket and couldn't wait to get home to put it on my car and finish the job. Before we got back, we stopped to buy some paint and another brush; I was raring to go.

A day or two later I said, "Mom, look at the car I just finished. It's a '61 Mercury. Isn't this the coolest car ever," as I proudly displayed all of my handiwork? "Son, it is beautiful, but I thought you said that you were missing an axle, and this car has both of them," she said. Her voice suddenly sounded stern. "Did you take it from another car when we were at Garrett's last Saturday? Son, if you did, you know that is stealing, don't you?"

I was mortified. I felt my heart sink into my chest, and for a moment couldn't get the words out of my mouth to respond. "Yes, Mom, I did take it. I'm sorry, but I just wanted my car to be perfect," I said, knowing in my heart that I had done wrong. "Well, son, we are going to have to take it back right now to Mr. Garrett, and you will have to tell him what you did." I couldn't believe it. First I stole something, and now I have to apologize in person. What could be worse?

So, Mom and I headed back to Garrett's Drugs, and I carried the axle with me in my pocket, this time with a less lofty goal—having to give it back and admit to Mr. Garrett that I was a thief. This was the most difficult thing I have ever had to do in my young life!

"Hello, Mr. Garrett," I said nervously, my hand shaking as I reached into my pocket to retrieve the missing axle. Then I explained the entire story to Mr. Garrett. "I am very sorry that I stole this axle from your store, and I will never do that again, I promise." He looked me right in the eye. I seriously thought my goose was cooked. "Mike," he said, "it takes a real man to tell the truth and admit a mistake, and

I'm proud of you for doing that. In fact, Mike, you were such a good boy to tell the truth that you can keep the axle." I couldn't believe what I was hearing.

I was relieved that my ordeal was over. Mom and I left the store, and I could tell that she wasn't mad at me anymore, though in fact she had never been mad at me in the first place but rather, as she said, "disappointed." Not only was Mom not mad, but I actually thought she was proud of me for owning up to what I had done.

When we finally arrived home, I hurried back up to my room and put the axle back on my car, but I have to admit I felt a strange combination of feelings. First, I was ashamed that I had stolen something, and at the same time, happy that I made it right. I realized later in life that Mom was trying to teach me a lesson that day, and she knew all along what she was going to do to make an impression on my young mind. "Son, I'm proud of you," Mom said, as she gave me a big hug. "Now you have learned that stealing is a very bad thing, and I know you will be a good boy and never do it again."

One of the most important lessons that any parent can teach a child is the difference between right and wrong. After that fateful day, that fact was not lost on me.

Lesson Number Eight: No Model Car Is Worth Committing a Sin to Build.

The impact of our parents on both Steve and I was unquestionable. It pains me that in today's society we seem to have lost our familial rudder. Life can often be quite difficult, and I have great empathy for parents rearing children these days. Many children who grow up in single-parent households where the parent has to work long hours just to be able to put food on the table, or other children who lack the direction and guidance of active and involved parents, have challenges. Some of these include learning right from wrong, how to navigate life's ups and downs, and making the right choices, to name a few. While it is a most difficult task, the rewards for those parents who take great care in being involved in their children's lives and strive to do the best job possible can be tremendous. To watch them become solid, productive, caring, and compassionate adults is a real gift from God. It would be hard to overstate the wonderful feeling of pride when children grow into adulthood in this manner.

For Steve and me, growing up in the 1950s was for sure a simpler time. There were no video games, social media, or even high-definition televisions. I remember so very well those days when televisions were always in black and white, and there were only three channels, ABC, NBC, and CBS. We had to rely on our imaginations and friends to occupy our free time after school and on the weekends.

Steve and I were doing what most young boys were at the time— playing cowboys and Indians, building tree houses and model cars, and riding our bicycles. But Steve couldn't always keep up with me because he had a disease that affected his legs called Perthes disease, also known as Legg-Calve-Perthes disease, which is a childhood disorder that affects the head of the femur and can break down and soften the bone. Steve had to wear a brace, walked with crutches, and sometimes even had to get around using a wheelchair. His leg was literally out of commission for at least three to four years of his young life beginning when he was just four years old. At the time there was no cure for the condition, and Mom and Dad prayed daily that God would heal Steve, and he would be able to walk again.

Thankfully, he eventually did.

I guess you could say that I was a protective older brother and looked out for Steve on a daily basis. I remember the time when our neighbor—the proverbial mean kid who lived next door—stomped on a new toy that Dad had just bought us. I was furious! "Steve, I'm going to whip that kid for breaking our toy," I said, as I grabbed my brother by the arm and headed next door to teach that bully a lesson. As Steve held him firmly on the ground, I gave him an old-fashioned butt whippin', and that seemed to do the trick. He never bullied us again.

Lesson Number Nine: Sticking Up for Those You Love Helps You Learn Teamwork and Crisis Management.

That lesson was always paramount in my early life, as it is today. As I look back on those early years, when childhood experiences play a part of whom we become as adults, one of my fondest and most precious of memories revolves around Christmas.

And, like most children all around the world, Steve and I loved the Christmas season, not so much for its religious implications, although in our family they were paramount, but for the gifts that we knew we would always receive. Sometimes Steve and I would jump the gun a bit in terms of finding and opening our presents, and when we did, we sure heard about it from Mom and Dad. One example of our youthful enthusiasm was the time that our parents thought that they had hidden our presents under the pull out couch that we had in our living room, well out of sight. Of course, we knew they were there and made it our mission to open up all of our toys the night *before* Christmas. The one thing about Christmas that was completely lost on us at the time was that Mom and Dad relished watching Steve and me open all of our gifts under the tree early on Christmas morning. We had disappointed them by opening up the gifts the night before, and we knew that by their reactions when they saw all of the torn-up wrapping paper strewn across the shag carpet. Our childhood impatience stole their joy, and we could see that clearly on our parents' sullen faces.

Lesson Number Ten: Patience Is a Virtue. Some Things in Life Are Better Experienced in Due Time.

Despite that youthful lapse in judgment, the Christmas season always brings back such wonderful memories for me and my brother. Like all children, we fondly recall the smells of the pine needles on our Christmas tree and the sweet aroma of cookies baking in the oven. Mom and Dad would read us Christmas stories before we went to bed and would actually make us ice cream made out of snow to add to the holiday fun.

But one of the happiest times Steve and I ever had at Christmas was the time we got our first bicycles thanks to my parents and two very special neighbors at the time.

The truth is Dad and Mom never had enough money to buy us brand-new bicycles. That's one of the reasons that I loved to go over and visit Leland and Shirley Hedges, a young couple who lived on Elberta Street, which is about five or six blocks away from our house and just down the street from the church. Dad always told us, "Boys, work comes first, and then you can go out and play." So on many days when we got out of Woodbine Elementary School, we would walk from the school to the church, where Dad was working on a sermon for the following Sunday. There we would finish our homework, and then I would walk down to the Hedges' house, hoping Leland would allow me to ride his bike. He owned a different-looking bike that I just loved to ride. It was an English bike, the one that had three working gears. Back then, we mostly rode American bikes, which had no gears but, as most kids my age would remember, they were very hard to ride up hills without completely becoming out of breath. That's why I loved Mr. Hedges's English bike more than anything else in my young life at the time.

So, one Christmas later, and much to my surprise, my dream finally came true. Steve and I woke up on Christmas morning to the most wonderful presents we had ever received—two bicycles. The only problem was that one of them was a shiny, new American bike and the other a used English bike, one that looked strangely familiar. Of course I just had to have the English one, but Dad thought that the only fair way to determine who would get which bike would be to toss a coin. "Boys, I'm going to flip a coin, and whoever gets tails can pick which bike they want." I was filled with anxiety, my heart beating out of my chest! As Dad flipped the coin, I held my breath in anticipation, and, wouldn't you know it, Steve won the coin toss. I was crushed. Then, in an instant, my world was rocked again when Steve chose the brand-spanking-new American bike. The English bike was finally mine. Hallelujah!

As Steve sat on his shiny new bike before taking it out for a spin, I grabbed my old English bike, running my fingers across the weathered, but functional, three gears. It felt like heaven. "Dad, where did you ever find an English bike like this? It must have been really expensive," I asked him, thinking about how blessed I was to have received such a wonderful present under the Christmas tree. "Son, Mr. Hedges gave me his bike, because he knew how much you enjoyed riding it and thought you would love to have it as a Christmas present." I knew in my heart at that moment that Mr. Hedges was a very special man.

Lesson Number Eleven: Shiny and New Isn't Always the Best Choice.

My brother and I were so fortunate to have such involved and loving parents. But we were also blessed to have both sets of grandparents actively involved in our lives and living nearby. Sadly, today, so many families are split up by fathers and mothers having to work far away from their hometowns, and as a result, the close-knit family unit is often disenfranchised. Rather than sharing their lives in person, they have to keep in touch virtually, using Skype or social media to stay connected. It is just an unfortunate by-product of our culture.

But when we were growing up, our grandparents were a vital part of our childhood; the impact they had on us was enormous.

Since Mom and Dad both worked full time jobs, in addition to pastoring a fledgling church, we stayed a lot with Mom's parents—Noble and Maggie Carson. We would spend endless hours at their house after school, on the weekends, and during the summer when school was out. Pop Carson was a prince of a man who worked his entire life on the railroad. He never had a lot of money but had a heart as big as the entire state of Tennessee. He and my grandmother lived in a tiny one-thousand-square-foot home with only two bedrooms on Glencliff Road.

They had three daughters—Montelle (my mother), Ruth, and Mary. They were each seven years apart. They also had two sons, Ray and Joe. All of the girls slept in the one tiny bedroom and my grandparents in the other, with Ray and Joe sleeping on a daybed in their small kitchen.

When Mom and Dad first got married, they needed a place to stay, so Pop and Grandmother offered them their bedroom. Pop Carson slept with the boys, Ray and Joe, on the daybed in the kitchen, while Grandmother Carson moved into the small bedroom with Ruth and Mary. My Pop and Grandmother Carson were two of the kindest, most giving people I have ever known.

Lesson Number Twelve: It Is More Blessed to Give than to Receive!

And, best of all, they had a television! Steve and I would go over to Pop's house many days to watch one of the three channels they had on their black and white TV. It was the main source of our entertainment at the time, and not only that, but grandmother would feed us, too. And did she ever feed us! She was an amazing cook, and while she would be preparing food in the kitchen, Pop would read us Bible stories and then turn on the television so we could watch our favorite shows, including *Zorro, Fury, The Big Show, My Friend Flicka,* and *Have Gun Will Travel,* whose popular character Paladin was my favorite and was played by the actor Richard Boone. My Aunt Mary, or as we called her, Witsie, and Uncle Joe were just like a brother and sister to me, and we would always bicker over what show to watch. Witsie always wanted to watch *American Bandstand,* and I, naturally, wanted to watch one of my western or action shows. To this day we laugh about which one of us was Pop's favorite based upon who would get to watch his TV show first.

Pop was a godly man, too. What I mean was he was deeply religious and read the Bible each and every day, taught an adult Sunday school class at our church, and prayed daily. Even though none of our four grandparents had a college education, they were rich in the knowledge of living life with principles, values, and faith. For several of my growing-up years, they all resided next door to each other and were close to us, too. They lived in small and well-kept homes on one-half acre lots on the outer edges of Woodbine on Elberta Street, directly across from our church in Nashville. Grandpop Lawson H. Hardwick, Sr. was a homebuilder. Though he often had to travel to where he could find work—to North Dakota on one occasion and to Florida on another, for example, he would always be there for his family and never once failed to support them monetarily. Grandmother Hardwick held a series of odd jobs, such as being a teacher in a kindergarten class or working as a piano teacher, but still, she was always there for us as well.

Both of our grandparents always had gardens, where they grew many of the vegetables that we always enjoyed. Pop Carson had a small backyard garden, and I can remember it vividly even today. He grew beans, tomatoes and okra, and what he didn't grow he would supplement by buying at the local farmer's market. When the vegetables were ready to pick, we would sit together in the backyard and shell the peas, snap the beans, shuck the corn, and put them in containers to store and freeze for the winter. There was no waste, and every dollar had to be stretched to go a long way. Pop never threw away anything!

He was fastidious, too, and knew how to fix everything, saving money by repairing all of his appliances and even his old lawnmower, which he fixed and refixed so many times to keep it working and in tip-top shape. I loved Pop Carson more than words can say. That's why in May 1990, I experienced the first devastating loss of my young adult life.

It was a very hot and sunny afternoon in Nashville with the temperature well into the scorching nineties, and Pop was working in his garden like always, when he suddenly, out of the blue, fell to the ground. He clutched his chest, as the pain was gripping and unbearable. In only a few more minutes, he would pass away from a massive heart attack. When Grandmother Carson found him, he was slumped over in the middle of his garden with the old tiller still running. When I heard the news, I was devastated. I was thirty years old at the time, and the thought of him being gone was just too much for me to bear. The next day I raced over to their house to see where he fell, and immediately went into the garden; the old tiller was still up against the fence where it had continued to run until it was out of gas. Next to their house was a small detached garage, and there I spotted Pop's old lawnmower. I touched it ever so gently, but still the rust and paint were peeling off of it everywhere, and I thought to myself, *I love Pop with all of my heart, but he and I are so very different. If this was my lawnmower, I wouldn't want to let my friends see it in that condition. I would have too much pride.* That was my "selfish" thought at the time.

The next day the funeral was held for Pop. It was one of the most emotional moments of my life, and I will never forget the words that Associate Pastor Scott said at the service: "He was as good a man as I have ever known." Those words were forever lodged in my memory. Pop Carson *was* a good man. Later that day, and after the service, we all went back to Pop's house. It was the place where I spent so much of my childhood, and now I was there without one of the two people who made it a home—my Pop. As we all sat on the sofa, I noticed Pop's Bible sitting on top of the coffee table. Pop would sit up every night on that sofa and read it, and I thought how sad it was that he would never have the chance to do it again. So I picked up the Bible and noticed his prayer list inside the front page. He had a long list of people for whom he was praying. So many of the names on that list were folks I knew very well. One was for a man who lost his wife, another for a woman who had a sick child, and the list went on and on. But something really struck me as I read through them. And that was the list of missing children that Pop was praying for each and every night, and that he copied from all of his used milk cartons. (Back then, pictures of missing children were listed on the back of each milk carton that was sold.) It was the beginning of corporate philanthropy, I would realize as I got much older.

He never personally knew any of those children pictured on those old milk cartons. They were complete strangers. But to Pop, they were all children of God, and they needed help. All he knew was that they were in danger. He hoped his daily prayers on their behalf would bring them back home to their loving families. Pop was a *good* man and a *godly* man.

Most of all, he, my parents, and grandparents laid the foundation for me, Steve, and my cousins to live a life rich in purpose and values that have stood the test of time. With each life lesson they so patiently taught us, we were blessed to receive their words of wisdom. For sure we tested them along the way, but without them, who knows where we would be or who we would become?

Lesson Number Twelve: Family Is a Source of Wisdom and Love, Providing the Foundation for a Purposeful and Meaningful Life.

CHAPTER 2

The Power of Parents:
The Reverend and Mrs. Hardwick

> All a child's life depends on the ideal it has of its parents. Destroy that and everything goes, morals, behavior, everything. Absolute trust in someone else is the essence of education.—E. M. Forster, *Where Angels Fear to Tread*

There have been numerous studies over the years about the role that parents play in development of their children. Diana Baumrind, who is a well-known clinical and developmental psychologist at the University of California, Berkeley, has written extensively about this subject. She has found that the best parents are those who are actively involved and responsive and who have high expectations for their children, yet still respect their autonomy. She said, "Authoritative parents generally raise children who do better academically, psychologically and socially than children whose parents are either too permissive or less involved, or controlling and more involved."

Having four children of my own—all of whom are, thankfully, well-adjusted and successful, as well as being an actively involved parent myself, I can attest to Baumrind's thesis. But everything I have learned about being a good and engaged parent I have learned from two of the best—the Reverend and Mrs. Hardwick.

Dad and Mom both came from very humble roots. They were salt of the earth Americans, caring and self-effacing people who had

21

tremendous empathy for others. What they did not have in material wealth, however, they more than made up by their wealth of heart and spirit. Mom worked so hard during most of my childhood and teenage years. She toiled during the day working in a series of public service jobs, as well as being an owner/operator of a kindergarten. And then, in the evenings, she would assume the role of a pastor's wife and attend to the needs of the parishioners, not to mention caring for two very active boys. I bet if I were to add up all the hours that both Mom and Dad worked during an average week, it would be well over eighty! But despite Mom's work ethic and her responsibilities at home and on the job, Steve and I were her main mission and priority. Not just during our childhood either. Until the day Mom passed, she would call my brother and me on the telephone each and every day, sometimes to tell us about a funny story, but mostly just to check in and see how we were doing. Now while some people might find that a bit intrusive and overbearing, I looked forward to hearing Moms' voice and was comforted knowing how much she cared.

Though there was this one time!

I was about seventeen years old and was dating a young lady named Becky, who I really was crazy about. We went bowling on that hot summer night in July at the Thompson Lane Bowling Alley on the south side of Nashville. Even though I knew I had a curfew, there were those occasions—like this one night where I just lost track of time and was later coming home than both of my parents would have liked. After I dropped my date off at her house I returned home, very quietly putting my key in the door so as not to wake up Mom or Dad. I was hoping no one would notice that I missed the mark by over two hours. Boy was I wrong! "Mike, is that you?" Mom asked, as I felt my heart sink into my chest. "Yes, Mom, I'm home, and I'm sorry if I'm a little late. I promise I won't do that again."

That has always been among my worst feelings, knowing that I let my parents down, even if it was for a simple thing like being late after a date. "Mike, Dad is asleep downstairs in our bedroom, so we can talk, right?" Here it comes. The question no son ever wants to have to discuss with his mother, especially at seventeen years old! "Son, how did your date go? Did you give her a kiss goodnight? Is Becky a good kisser?" As we sat down on the sofa, I felt a sense of calm, knowing Mom loved me to death and was sincerely interested in knowing how I felt about this particular young lady. "Mike," Mom said as she leaned in toward me, her arms outstretched and with a twinkle in her eye, "You know, if you don't kiss the girls during a date, you are not normal."

Not normal? I thought, as I took a deep breath, my heart beating like a drum. *I must be very normal*, I thought to myself, because I in fact, did kiss Becky, and quite a good bit, I might add.

"Mom," I said, "it was great. Really great! First we had fun going bowling, and then I had even more fun when I kissed her." Mom's sweet face told the story. She just smiled, gave me a kiss on the cheek, and then she went back downstairs to bed.

Mom was never happy until she knew that Steve and I were safe in our beds, no matter what time it was or what went on in her day. She was my best friend all of my life, but, more importantly, she was also the most involved, loving, and greatest mom any son could have.

I came to realize over the years that her midnight questions were a way for Mom to keep up with us boys. While both Mom and Dad could have stayed up late and been negative in how they approached either of their sons returning late from a date and missing their curfew, they chose a positive path instead. Mom was not just interested in being a concerned and caring mom but a great and supportive friend, too.

This positivity was evident in how they lived their entire lives and in almost everything they did.

I vividly recall a story Dad told us boys when we were younger and also many times throughout our adult lives. It was never a stale tale, and I think about it often as an example of Dad's embracing the positive aspects of life, and having faith that the negatives are transient experiences that can provide a great basis for reflection and learning.

Dad, in addition to being a brilliant pastor, and loving father, was also a visionary. He had a knack for knowing what would be the next big thing and had the chutzpa to tackle it with unbridled enthusiasm.

Our little church on Elberta Street was growing like a weed in the early 1970s. Dad knew that in order to keep the momentum going, he needed to acquire more land and move from a half-acre space to a larger parcel of land and in an area of Nashville that was up and coming. He was very excited to have acquired five acres of land about five to six miles farther south of the city on Old Hickory Boulevard. His plan was to save up enough money to eventually build a larger church that could provide enough space for additional Sunday school classrooms, a fellowship hall for church socials and dinners, and more seating capacity in the auditorium to add new parishioners.

Two years later, Dad decided to finally build the new sanctuary, which would allow up to six hundred people to worship comfortably. There was one slight problem. Dad needed to raise the money for construction. That's when he came up with a novel idea! That was to sell church bonds. He was a salesman by nature, so offering these bonds to the public in order to finance the sanctuary seemed like an easy undertaking. His concept was to sell $100, $500, and $1,000 bonds so he could raise the $400,000 he needed to complete the construction. Sadly for Dad, no one was buying.

To further compound the problem Dad needed to sell the Elberta Street church property as well, but, sadly, it was just not generating much interest from possible buyers at all.

Dad's brother-in-law—Bob Clement, who was on the Tennessee Public Service Commission at the time and later served as a member of the US House of Representatives and was married to my aunt, Witsie, heard about Dad's dilemma and offered to help.

"Now, Brother Hardwick, I do want to help you. We both know that we have to start with the church members and families first, and then we can call on people outside of the church," Bob said. "I'll also do everything I can to push the church bonds because I believe in you, the church mission, and what a difference you have made in other people's lives. I will never forget what you've done to help rehabilitate prisoners. I don't think anyone in Tennessee would ever forget that you were with my father when he was governor on that day when he commuted the sentences of those prisoners who were on death row to ninety-nine years. I still remember you telling me about the photo of you and my dad as you offered up a prayer for those prisoners, and which actually showed up in newspapers in Australia!"

Dad was thrilled to have Bob's help and told him, "Bob, I would appreciate it, and I want to thank you for your kindness."

Bob, and only a few other potential investors, attended a meeting to learn about why the bonds would be a good investment. On that Friday afternoon of the meeting, it was overcast and rainy, and not many people showed up, which was a huge disappointment for both of my parents, and Bob as well. Still, Dad gave it his all and, as usual, delivered a passionate and intelligent presentation. He didn't sell one darned bond!

Disappointed and dejected, Dad drove his car from downtown Nashville back out to the church, hoping that being there would boost his spirits. Here's how he recalls the story: "It was a very rainy, dreary afternoon, and I stopped at a red light and was feeling so downcast and felt for a minute as though the old devil himself was sitting right next to me in the car. Then, as I turned my head, I noticed the old city cemetery on the opposite side of the street. Hundreds of tombstones were lined up methodically in a row, which certainly didn't lift my spirits!

"I began to wonder if I may have made a bad decision to buy land and build a larger church building and take the church into debt. It was as if the old devil caused me to question whether I was doing this just to make a name for myself. I thought, *What a fool you are; you are so young and have your entire future ahead of you, and here you are putting the church into potential financial peril!* As the light changed, I headed over to the church, but when I arrived, no one was there, which only served to make me feel even more alone. So I drove back home, had dinner with Mom and you boys, and the three of you went to bed. I couldn't sleep and was really worrying about how to get the church back on the right path. After awhile I began to pray, and I basically spoke out loud saying to the Lord, 'I believe, Lord, you directed me to build this new church building, and I'm not selfishly doing it for my own personal reasons.' I continued telling the Lord that if I was right, then it was really *His* problem. After that little personal prayer meeting, I went to bed and was finally able to easily and more quickly fall asleep. God had settled my soul, at least for that moment."

About a week later, Dad was feeling slightly better, yet he was still quite worried about how to get the church out of the problem, for he felt so responsible. He was home one night when he got a phone call from Bill Smithson, one of our church members and a businessman in town, who was a very good friend of Dad's and was well aware of the situation. "Brother Hardwick, have you sold all of our church bonds yet, and if you haven't, then how many of them do you have left?"

Dad replied, "Bill, we have only sold a few, and frankly I am very worried about the whole situation."

"Well, Brother Hardwick, I have some good news. My business is doing very well at present. I'll buy them all from you, and at their full price, too."

"Are you serious, Bill? You want to buy them all? That would cost you a bundle of money."

Bill reaffirmed that he did, indeed, want to purchase all of the remaining church bonds, and Dad, of course, was thrilled. Also, that same week a buyer contracted to purchase the Elberta Street church property at full price! Dad's thought was, *The good Lord has answered my prayer!* Thanks to Bill Smithson's generosity and the old Elberta Street property selling, Dad was able to build the new church sanctuary and finally have his dream fulfilled.

Dad told us this story many times over the years to illustrate a very important life lesson for us, and that was the importance of having a positive attitude and faith in the face of trouble, regret, and disappointment, knowing that the grace and love of God will prevail. He taught us the power of doing the right thing and then trusting God for the outcome. This has helped me throughout my life, especially the one time many years later when I faced my own battle with personal despair and financial loss.

In addition to being a perpetually positive person, Dad was also funny. Actually he was quite hysterical! (Mom was also known for her practical jokes, by the way.)

Many people might find this surprising, but pastors—especially my dad—had a wicked sense of humor as well as tremendous compassion for others, as you would expect most pastors to have. And that was a real blessing as it turned out, too. Imagine spending each and every day listening to people's problems—Miss Lou's trouble with gout, Joe's battle with the bottle, Billy's breakup with his wife of forty years. Even for a man of God, this can be a tough way to make a living, at least to my way of thinking. But Dad was cut from a different cloth. When he would pastor to inmates as chaplain at the Tennessee State Penitentiary, he would give even the most evil people—murderers, rapists, and more—a dose of his wit, humor, and compassion. (By the way, Dad was appointed to that position by Tennessee Governor Frank G. Clement, Bob Clement's father.)

Dad would try to give peace and comfort to even the most hardened criminals and throw in a touch of his subtle humor as well. "Now, Jimmy, I know you have sinned, and killing your wife was surely a terrible offense against her and God. But things sure could be worse. You could have married someone you really didn't like."

Then there was a more serious story of another preacher's son. He was a sort of quiet kid who was well-educated and never got into any serious trouble. The red-haired son of a Methodist minister, he got into some very big trouble by being an accomplice to one of the most heinous of crimes in East Tennessee at the time. Dad offered to counsel him while he was locked up in prison when Dad served as prison chaplain.

What happened? One night one of his buddies talked him into driving him to the local convenience store in town, where his friend was hoping to steal some money, something he didn't know about at the time. As he waited in his car for his friend to return with some bread and milk, he heard a shot fired. It left him cold.

When his friend raced back to the car, hoping to make a clean and fast getaway, he asked him, "My God, what happened? Did you just shoot that guy? I thought you were just going to get a few groceries!"

"Don't ask me any more questions; let's get out of here, now!" The young man was so frightened that he couldn't think straight, and put his foot to the gas pedal with as much full force as an atom bomb. The two fugitives drove away.

Two hours later, the store owner died.

Following a salacious trial, the young man sat in his cold and barren prison cell knowing that he had actually killed a fellow human being, or at least played a part in it. When Dad paid him a visit, he asked him this one simple question: "Son why did you do this?"

"I don't know, Reverend, I made a very terrible decision, and I don't know how to explain it. I guess you could say it was just my one moment of crazy," he told Dad with his voice quivering and sadness in his eyes.

Dad said to him, "Son, life is not just about one singular event, either positive or negative. It is a series of countless decisions one makes, but you can become either a bitter person or a better person. It is your choice now how to respond." That was quintessential Reverend Hardwick.

Dad knew that anyone can change his or her life with the help and direction of the Lord; he saw it firsthand most of his own career. But, he also knew the power of education and self-reflection, not to mention faith, to be able to live a fulfilled and purposeful life.

Another one of the major attributes both Mom and Dad shared passionately was their love for and belief in education. Books were as integral to our lives as food, water, and shelter. They were everywhere in our house, too. And not just on the bookshelves. They were sitting on coffee tables, night stands, on the kitchen table, and even in the one car we had during most of my childhood. To this day, Dad wakes up early every morning and reads the *Nashville Tennessean*, our local newspaper, literally cover to cover. As a child, and young adult, I can still remember Dad sitting in the den late at night reading anything he could get his hands on for hours at a time. There were history books, political books, books of all kind. His mind was a repository of political, religious, business, and philosophical observations and truisms.

That might have been one of the reasons that when Dad prepared a thirty-minute sermon, it would quite literally take him twenty hours of study and preparation. Every word, every syllable, every inflection of his voice was carefully thought out and prayed over, so that when Sunday morning came around, Dad could easily deliver what the Lord had helped him prepare. What he spoke he knew, and what he cared about in his message mattered, because Dad was willing to invest the significant amount of hours and prayer each and every week for sixty years to lead his flock into the presence of the Lord. He always felt a tremendous responsibility to not just wing it but rather be a great teacher and source of sound biblical information and leadership.

I always tell people, "Dad is a great preacher, and an even greater pastor!"

I have tried to follow both of my parents' examples in rearing my own children—Shayna, Megan, Lawson, and Michael. My wife, Stephanie, shares my belief that providing our children with a sound education and surrounding them with a loving environment at home based on solid biblical values is the cornerstone of success in life. For that I am eternally grateful.

I subscribe to the belief that my primary role as a parent is to be a great mentor and teacher to my children. While I love being their friend, that has always been a secondary role for me. I have always tried to maintain real consistency in how I loved and taught my children so that they would never doubt or wonder what I believed about most things. When there isn't a clear message, then confusion can begin to set in and cause them to make poor decisions. At the same time, I've always wanted my children to grow into what God wants them to be, not just what I desire.

One of our family traditions, and one which I highly recommend, is spending one-on-one time with your children and doing that each and every year. With four children, this can be a very time-consuming effort but to me it has meant the world. From snow skiing trips, golf outings, European cultural tours, and weeks on end at the lake, the memories we made are priceless.

I've also tried to create seminal moments, like Mom and Dad did for Steve and me for most of our young lives. Every year the entire family goes on what we call "family snow ski trips," where we take the entire week and ski in places such as Deer Valley, Vail, Lake Tahoe, and others. I also take Shayna and Megan on annual father/daughter trips where we visit places they would like to see such as New York City, Portland and the great Northwest, Napa Valley, Palm Beach, and even France! The girls always get to pick the location of where we will all go, at which hotels we will stay, and the fun side trips and other vacation activities. (We actually began doing these trips when the girls were only twelve or thirteen, and even with them both now married, they still insist on our father/daughter trips.) My sons and I look forward to our yearly adventures, too, and we fondly refer to them as "Hardwick boys ski trips." We have so enjoyed skiing at some really special and beautiful places such as Taos, Heavenly, Vail, and Whistler in Canada. We began doing these snow ski trips when Lawson was just a little boy. We even taught Dad how to snow ski when he was a young fifty years old. He still wants to tag along!

Another example of these special moments is the time Lawson graduated from college, and I wanted to do something for him that would be out of the ordinary. Like any father, I was so proud of him. Lawson graduated from Lee University with a degree in business. He went there on a math scholarship, which, thankfully, saved us more than a little money for tuition.

So this is what I planned for Lawson. I've always loved the Jewish tradition of having a bar mitzvah, marking the coming of age of a young man. While traditionally this is done for boys when they turn thirteen years old, Lawson was now twenty-two, so I copied a novel idea from my good friend Dave Ramsey, which I had been fortunate to be able to participate in for Dave's son, Daniel, a year or so earlier. I knew Lawson would love and cherish this idea.

I invited forty of my closest friends, family, and colleagues to our home who I thought could offer Lawson great advice as he was moving on to the next chapter of his life. Over two nights, each man brought a book that meant a lot to him and inscribed some of his pearls of wisdom inside. I asked each one to speak to Lawson for about five minutes and give him words of encouragement and wisdom. It was certainly one of the best experiences for Lawson and is something neither of us will ever forget. I am eternally grateful for all of the men who took part in this meaningful event, and since that time, many of the men who were there have done the same thing for their own boys.

This experience reminds me of a great quote by the late Dr. Martin Luther King Jr.: "The function of education is to teach one to think intensively and to think critically; intelligence plus character—that is the goal of true education."

In addition to the written and spoken word, endless study and devotion to their children, church, and the community, Mom and Dad were also as much influenced by music as they were by the written and spoken word.

The Greek philosopher Plato said, "Music is a moral law. It gives soul to the universe, wings to the mind, flight to the imagination, and charm and gaiety to life and to everything." I tend to agree with him!

Mom and Dad found joy, and both excelled in music—Mom on the piano and accordion, and Dad on the bass fiddle, banjo, and mandolin, as well as the baritone horn. Dad was so good, in fact, that the Nashville Symphony Orchestra invited him to join when Dad was just in his late teenage years, but he chose the ministry instead. In high school, Dad was a scrawny 135 pounds, but he was the best and most commanding drum major in the band in his school's history. (Well, at least that is what he tells us.)

Still, the music filled our home with melodious bliss as long as I can remember. Mom would make us practice the piano each and every day. "Mike and Steve, you two get down here right now; it's time for your piano practice," Mom would say, as she got our sheet music ready for us to practice. Like most boys, I really wanted to be outside playing ball with my friends, not practicing the piano! Even worse, we had to take lessons twice weekly. But, once I got over the fact that I had to practice, I truly enjoyed my music lessons. Our piano teacher was legally blind, but she could feel and hear the music more than anyone else I ever knew. She and our parents instilled in us the love of sound, and that has been an integral part of my life to this day. (In fact, one of my two undergraduate degrees was in music.)

Who knew, that before Backstreet Boys and the Jonas Brothers, there were the Hardwick Boys. Dad, Steve, and I formed a trio of sorts, and we would perform at church almost every week. I was a baritone; Steve was the lead singer, and Dad, of course, with his booming voice and almost perfect pitch, the tenor. We sang songs such as, "I Won't Have to Cross Jordan Alone," "The King Is Coming," and "I'll Fly Away!" I must admit we were pretty darned good; at least that is what the wonderful folks at the church made us think. So much so that when old Sister Floyd passed away, her family asked the Hardwick Boys to sing at her funeral. For more than forty years, we sang together in church services, at weddings and funerals, in church conferences all across the country, even getting Mom and Grandmother Hardwick in the act too. There were many Sundays when we would sing, Mom would play the piano, and Grandmother Hardwick would accompany us on the organ.

My most challenging and difficult performance beyond a shadow of a doubt was to perform at Mom's funeral. She passed away in 2006 from kidney failure, and thirty-five hundred people packed Christ Church to express their sorrow and love for this most amazing woman.

Mom had wanted *her boys* to sing her favorite song, "I Won't Have to Cross Jordan Alone." "Son, you have got to do what Mom wanted, and we will do it one last time for her," Dad told me, knowing that I was having a hard time with her loss. Somehow Steve and I finally pulled ourselves together and got up the courage to sing. The moment we managed to complete the last note, we all broke down in tears and hugged each other right there in front of thirty-five hundred friends.

The hallmark of my parents and the core of our family, and what I try to convey to my own children and grandchildren, is the power of faith and love. Baseball great Jackie Robinson once said: "A life is not important except in the impact it has on other lives." I can say with great pride that my parents have literally had tremendous and lasting positive impact on the lives of thousands.

Mom and Dad truly loved each other, too. Mom believed in and trusted Dad, and he, in turn, relied on her to keep him on track. They were the love of each other's lives. I believe they learned how to love so deeply from their parents, as well. I have heard my father quote Grandmother Carson often. She would say, "Brother Hardwick, if you can't win people through love, then you probably can't win them."

I must say that Mom and Dad's hard work and love for us had a great impact on me. I saw them live what they preached, not just on Sunday but every other day of the week in front of others and in the privacy of our home. They were consistent in their parenting and viewed the family unit as their priority, and they took great pains to codify their strategy. They also had a firm foundation from their own parents and learned from them how to love their family, other people, and God. They were the most positive, funny, hard-working, loving, and talented two people I have ever known, and not just because they were my parents. I simply cannot imagine a more wonderful life than what God blessed me with to be a part of such an amazing family.

CHAPTER 3

The Church That Rev. Hardwick Built

Well done is better than well said.—Benjamin Franklin

Too often I've found that many folks talk the talk, but don't walk the walk. They will go on and on about this or that but never accomplish much of anything. One of my favorite old sayings echoes that idea: "After all is said and done, much tends to be said while little seems to be done!" This is further illustrated by an old Bible song that goes something like this: "It's not to he who runs the swiftest, nor to he who shines for a day, but he who endures, the same shall be saved."

Rev. Hardwick is that rare breed of a person who could do both. As the pastor of Christ Church for sixty years, he verbalized his thoughts and dreams until they became a part of his lexicon—he stayed the course regardless of the monotony of the task, just doing the right thing day after day, week after week, year after year. From a tiny church he built with his own sweat equity, with the help and hard work of so many others, to the largest in Nashville at the time with more than eight thousand parishioners, the church that Rev. Hardwick built laid the foundation for our family's future, emotional good fortune, and unwavering spiritual faith.

Over the years, people have often asked me what was the secret to Dad's success. After all, he grew up without a hefty trust fund, didn't have a father who handed him a thriving business, and lived in a rural southern community of essentially working-class people. But he had one thing that no money or position of power could ever buy, and that was faith.

Faith means many different things to many different people, but for Dad it was as much a part of his being as the steady beating of his heart. I believe my deep love for the church, as well as my commitment to the work of the church, came from him, as well as my mother and grandparents. They taught me one of the most important lessons of my life, and that is that God is love, that God deeply cares for all of us, and that we are expected to love one another. The Bible actually says in John 13:35: "By this all people will know that you are my disciples, if you have love for one another."

In the society we live in today, one filled with endless selfies, reality television, and social media, the church often takes a back seat, and I would argue it needs to be integrated more into our lives, and for this reason: it is perhaps the single greatest institution in the world today for good, and, at its core, gives believers a rock-solid foundation for living a life of love and meaning. Think of all the hospitals, universities, colleges, and museums, among many others, that would not exist without funding from the church. I am not talking about organized religion, but rather about the countless number of churches both large and small—all around the world—that truly just help people live meaningful lives every day. While the church as an institution does have its faults, its guiding principles help bring order to chaos, faith to naysayers, hope to the downtrodden, and love to those willing to embrace its core values.

Dad got his first taste of the power and the pull of God when he was just a child. He lived in the small southern town of Finley, Tennessee, and grew up in the 1930s and 1940s when there was not much to keep a young, spirited boy entertained. There were no bowling alleys, major sporting events, or even television, and there was only one tiny theater in town that showed one black and white movie at a time. This was hardly a stimulating environment for a young person, for sure.

Here's the story Dad often told about his little hometown of Finley, Tennessee, in an effort to evoke a laugh or two. When someone would ask him where he was from, he would say, "Have you ever heard of Dyersburg, Tennessee?" If they said, yes, he would then tell them, "Well, if you've heard of Dyersburg, then you surely must have heard of a suburb of Dyersburg called Finley."

"Oh, yes, I have heard of Finley," they would often say.

"Well, if you heard of Finley, then you surely have heard of a suburb of Finley called Cottonwood Point. That's where I'm from." (Cottonwood Point was a small village of probably no more than fifty or so folks on the banks of the mighty Mississippi River in the northwest corner of Tennessee.)

As Dorothy said in *The Wizard of Oz*, "There's no place like home," and there was no place like the old small house in which Dad was actually born, and which is still standing to this day even though it is abandoned and overgrown with weeds. I went back there in 2014 with most of my children and grandchildren along with Dad to spend a glorious weekend. Dad told us many stories about when he was a boy. He took us to the places where he played, went fishing with his friends, and spent so many hot summer afternoons doing "a whole lot of nothing," as he would often say.

During that visit, he led us down a very old country road where the paving turned into a gravel road that became the entrance to a very old cemetery. There we saw many graves of Dad's aunts and uncles who have long since passed away. One of the other highlights of the trip was having Dad baptize my youngest son, Michael, as well as Maggie, Steve's youngest daughter. We all stood around the old baptismal tank in the small church building that my grandfather Hardwick and great-grandfather Weidman built when my father was just five or six years old. What an amazing experience it was to be in that hallowed place watching Dad do what he does best!

Well, needless to say, with a population of no more than around 250 to 500 people, Finley was hardly a place that was a must-see destination for visitors. I believe it is accurate to say that there was very little or no excitement at all happening in that little country town in the 1930s, rather just good, honest, hardworking people who spent most of their lives just getting by.

But there *were* the traveling preachers! These were the bombastic, colorful, and mesmerizing men who traveled from town to town across the country putting on what was known back then as "tent revival meetings." These preachers provided uplifting spiritual messages and oftentimes did so with the showmanship of a circus ring leader. In the eighteenth and nineteenth centuries, these traveling evangelists set up their tents in the rural South and Midwest, accommodating the settlers as they moved across the country to build better lives for themselves. In the absence of bricks and mortar churches, these charismatic preachers served a great purpose by pitching a tent and preaching to anyone in need of spiritual guidance and healing.

It was during one of these tent revival meetings in Finley that Dad met the one and only Brother A. D. Gurley.

Dad remembers Brother Gurley as a rather striking man with dark, flowing hair and always impeccably dressed in a stark white suit. When he spoke, this dramatic and ecclesiastic firebrand was simply spellbinding. "Boys," Dad would tell Steve and me, "when I was a teenager, this was the only excitement we ever had in our small town. When I first met the traveling preacher, and he threw up his tent for three or four weeks, I was spellbound. When I got to know Brother Gruley and heard his message during those tent revival meetings, I felt the calling of the Lord in my young heart. I knew then what my calling was all about, and from that moment on I dedicated my life to the work of the Lord."

In the meantime, Pop Hardwick decided to move the family from Finley, Tennessee, to Nashville, when Dad was around twelve years old. Pop and Grandmother Hardwick joined the First United Pentecostal Church in West Nashville immediately after the move. It was there that this twelve-year-old, during his first time at church, met my mom, Montelle, who was just thirteen. Just six years later, Dad convinced her to marry him, and as they say, the rest is history.

Dad adapted to his new surroundings very well and gained notoriety as a talented musician. Though he was a skinny kid, he still loved playing football but didn't have the physical power to make the high school football team. His friends from his high school days have told us that he could play very well, was very fast, and even had a little mean streak in him. Even though he didn't get to play high school football, he did use his time wisely by developing his gift for music. Dad became interested in playing the bass fiddle and other string instruments and learned the baritone horn while playing in the Cohn High School band. He quickly became good at his music craft, so good, in fact, that he was named drum major for the high school band, a position of which he was very proud.

Regardless of his musical talent, Dad always knew he wanted to become a preacher. From his early experiences going to tent revivals as a boy, and listening intently to the many preachers who would stay at his home when they were in town, his heart was inspired and open to the call of God. He told us that the men he grew up admiring and looking up to were ministers. He loved listening to them preach and became very interested in studying the Bible, as a result. He said, "Son, I never doubted that call, and to this day, I am certain that is what God ordained me to do."

Another mentor in Dad's life was Brother W. M. Greer, who was the district superintendent for Tennessee's United Pentecostal Church (UPC). The UPC was created from the Pentecostal movement that began with a Bible school in Topeka, Kansas, in 1901, according to church history and with the Azusa Street Revival in Los Angeles, California, in 1906. The movement has its organizational roots back in 1916 when a group of Pentecostal ministers began to unite around the teaching of the oneness of God, and water baptism in the name of Jesus Christ. Today, the church serves nearly three million constituents from 201 nations, and has thousands of churches, practicing ministers, and missionaries around the world.

Dad became an ordained minister in this organization sometime around 1950. The UPC was organized by districts and sections. Each state represented a district, and the Tennessee District was further divided into nine sections. Each section had one sectional leader, and Dad was elected to be the sectional leader for Middle Tennessee while in his late twenties. Dad really looked up to Brother Greer as one of his longtime mentors who provided him so much inspiration. He was also impressed with his keen business sense, which was an anomaly, since most preachers lacked those skills that Dad recognized, even at an early age, would be necessary to build a successful church.

Dad went about doing what he felt he was supposed to do with his life. He kept slowly and steadily laboring to grow the church, initially in a very small, old building on the corner of Rose and Sadler Streets in 1949, which probably would seat no more than fifty to seventy-five people. When the state decided it wanted to put in a new interstate highway in 1956, right on the church's property, it gave Dad enough money to purchase an existing house on Elberta Street, which was on a slightly larger parcel of land and yet only a few blocks away from the Rose and Sadler Streets location. Dad and Grandfather Hardwick built a basement church building directly behind the house with their own hands, as I've mentioned before.

Over time, the house on Elberta Street was just too small to provide enough classroom space for our small but growing congregation. So, in 1960, we tore the house down and built another basement building in its place with classrooms and a fellowship hall, and then a couple of years later Dad built the 250-seat sanctuary on top of the basement buildings. The congregation kept growing and growing as word spread about Dad's preaching and all of the wonderful services the church provided to its worshipers. With such steady growth, it became clear that we had outgrown this space, too, so in 1976, Dad decided to move to Old Hickory Boulevard, where he constructed a new, beautiful, fifteen-thousand-square-foot building that would seat about six hundred people and had expanded space for larger classrooms and fellowship meetings. One interesting thing to note about that first church on Elberta Street was that Dad hired a young Nashville architect by the name of Bill

Shelton. Bill believed in his mission and, as a result, offered Dad his professional services for a very small price. He was so impressed with him that he used the young architect to design all of his other church buildings over the ensuing years.

With all of the growth and success of the church, it didn't take long for Dad to rise up the ranks of the UPC church hierarchy, and soon Dad became the sectional presbyter for Middle Tennessee, where he would often work with his mentor, Brother Greer, who by that time had even greater responsibility and leadership opportunities. In the role of presbyter, which comes from the Greek word that means the leader of a local group, Dad had about thirteen churches he would oversee in little Tennessee towns such as Dickson and Franklin, among others. Once or twice a year, the sectional presbyters would meet to discuss the business affairs of the Tennessee District as well. During one of those meetings, which Brother Greer led, an issue came up that pitted Dad against the other eight sectional presbyters, and the discussion became heated. "There was this resolution that I wanted to get passed, and low and behold, most of the other presbyters were against me," Dad said. "At the time I was young and full of vim and vinegar, and not much wisdom, I have to admit, but I lobbied hard for my position, and nothing I did was working. I was becoming more than a little irritated and frustrated and felt my blood pressure rise like the dickens."

As Dad was huffing and puffing around the room, a gentle nudge on the back of his shoulder made all of the difference. "Brother Hardwick," Brother Greer said, "How about you and me take a walk?" Dad was still fuming but knew in his heart he needed to calm down, and who better to help him do that than his friend and mentor Brother Greer? "Now, Brother Hardwick, one of the things I have learned in life is that I'm not always right. I've made a lot of mistakes. But here's what I have always said to myself, and now I will say it to you: keep your reverse gear in good working order, because sometimes it's okay to reverse your direction."

With those wise and soothing words from a man who captivated Dad as a very young and inexperienced pastor and continued to do when he was an adult, Dad calmed down and returned to the meeting ready and able to compromise. I've always tried to teach my children and employees the same thing—keep your reverse gear in good working order! (I have learned, just like Dad, the often painful lesson that I am not always right.)

As the years went by, our small church congregation continued its growth spurt. At the same time, around 1970, he was becoming more and more alienated from the UPC. He felt the teachings were becoming increasingly legalistic as the older leaders such as Brother Greer, whom he held so much respect and love for, were retiring, and younger leaders appeared to be more interested in gaining leadership positions within the organization. The organization became more and more ironfisted with hard-line positions designed, I believe, to exert control over people on things that just were silly, unreasonable, and certainly not biblically based, including: teaching that women should not cut their hair or wear shorts or pants, and parishioners should not attend movies or ballgames or go to movies! While Dad deeply loved and revered many of the older pastors such as Brothers Greer and Gurley, and he knew, as most do, that there is much to not like about the negative influences that come out of Hollywood in the form of movies and TV shows, he felt the younger pastors were imparting messages that he believed were simply not accurate and were full of unreasonable dogma. Dad was a man of strong values and principles. He was determined to lead his local congregation according to what he believed were biblically based teachings, not just one man's opinion.

This was one of those trying times that would test his resolve.

"Son," he told me, "I will not put those kinds of teachings on our congregation. It pains me greatly to do this, but I know we have to leave the UPC and become an independent church." That was a tough decision, and Dad knew once he declared his independence, he would be ostracized from the only church organization he had ever known or been a part of—one he dearly loved and grew in as a young pastor for well over twenty-five years. But this time he did not reverse gears, and

I firmly believe that his leaving the UPC was the best thing that ever happened to Dad. It forced him to branch out and meet other Evangelical pastors and leaders in the Christian church world. It also paved the way for the incredible growth and success of Christ Church and gave Dad a clean slate to build his own congregation.

With our newly found independence and growing recognition in Nashville, we once again found ourselves in need of a larger space for worship. In 1988, we built our next church structure, which had a large auditorium with seating for a whopping 2,220 people, more classrooms, a much larger fellowship hall, and even a new bookstore. Now Dad had the physical platform to preach with many more worshipers and deliver sermons that were true to God's word and delivered as only Dad could.

Our church was filled with people from all walks of life, too. There were absolutely no divisions by wealth or power. Everyone was equal in Dad's eyes. There were highly educated folks who attended Vanderbilt University, as well as university professors, lawyers, accountants, bankers, builders, school teachers, janitors, electricians, and plumbers. All of whom found our church a place where they could worship and grow in their walk with the Lord, while at the same time meeting so many different folks from all over Middle Tennessee from so many differing backgrounds. It was interesting that we had college professors who taught Sunday school classes in our church alongside my Pop Carson, though he never even graduated from high school. And there were folks from many other different socioeconomic backgrounds, as well. Dad and Mom never noticed the color of people's skin, where they came from, or what job they held. They loved them all just as intensely as they loved God. And they were not afraid to hear a wide range of opinions, even if they differed from their own. Dad would often bring in many associate pastors, sometimes who were even more powerful speakers than he and, regardless, gave them ample time to preach and learn the art of pastoring. My parents had tremendous love and respect for everyone, and I believe that came from their innate character and rock-solid belief system.

I must say that there was so much love in that one-hundred-thousand-square-foot church facility, and as the congregation steadily increased, in 2000 we knew we had to expand our space yet again. Dad decided to build an addition of another one hundred thousand square feet that included a large family/life gymnasium center, an incredible new children's interactive teaching center, many more classrooms, and a beautiful prayer tower. We even added a large church cemetery, where all of my grandparents and my mother are buried, as well as so many passed friends and church members from over these past sixty-plus years.

Through years of slow and steady growth, a solid business plan, and a charismatic and determined pastor, Christ Church became the most influential and successful church in all Nashville and much of the southeastern part of our country during that era. Despite that success, Dad and Mom never neglected to involve us boys in every aspect of the church—from mowing the church lawn, directing traffic in the parking lots, driving the church buses, teaching young adult classes, sitting on the church board of directors, and singing in the choir, to taking us on "vacations" focusing on Dad's preaching in revivals all over the South as well as other parts of the country; we were always part of their journey.

Our parents never left home without us, and, in fact, took us on almost every church-related trip they could. I vividly remember driving with our parents to California and seeing Disneyland for the first time, and taking a four-week summer driving trip in a rented Winnebago. The four of us, and both sets of grandparents, traveled together in that tiny Winnebago, driving along the southern route from Nashville all the way out through Dallas, Albuquerque, Phoenix, and on to California, then up the Pacific coastline north via Highway 1 to Portland, Oregon, then back home on the northern route through Salt Lake City, Denver, Kansas City, and St. Louis. We were able to see the beautiful blue waters of the Pacific, witness the majestic snowcapped Rocky Mountains, and see Old Faithful and the Gateway Arch, as well as many other things that make our great land so spectacular. We played board games with my grandparents while Dad drove us throughout the West, and laughed as both of my grandfathers told us old stories and jokes. What fun memories!

It was a blast being with my parents, brother, and grandparents as a young teenager. As we traveled, we usually toured two types of properties in particular that we all loved, those being churches and ballparks. I've tried to continue that tradition with my own children, too. They will tell you that their dad loves visiting old churches and cathedrals just like their grandfather, and, of course, any college and major league ballpark, too. I guess the apple doesn't fall far from the tree!

Traveling with our parents, and being such an integral part of their lives at home and at work, had a tremendous positive effect on Steve and me. As children, we never viewed our involvement in church work as hard work; we had so much fun doing it. From selling hot doughnuts and lunches door-to-door to watching my parents and grandparents live a life of service to God and others, I have been blessed to have had a front row seat to a fabulous and inspiring life. With small and steady steps—building one brick at a time—Dad was able to realize his dream and become a role model for not just our family, but for the thousands of people who were fortunate to know him as a pastor, friend, confidant, mentor, and leader.

A building is just a building if not for the love and determination of the people who make it come alive. The church that my dad, Rev. Hardwick, built was just that kind of place. No matter how large or small, how much or little square footage, it is a structure that will last forever. When the bricks begin to crumble, the wooden pews crack, and the lights dim, it will always shine bright in the hearts of thousands upon thousands of wonderful people and true believers.

It typically took Dad twenty hours of study and prayer to prepare a forty-five-minute sermon. But each of those forty-five-minute sermons will be cherished by those who were lucky enough to hear Dad preach. Every word, carefully conceived and executed, will, in my opinion, last a lifetime.

CHAPTER 4

My Coincidental Education:
From Theology to the Market

An investment in knowledge pays the best interest.
—Benjamin Franklin

Everyone in life has a calling. In many ways I thought mine would be fairly obvious and straightforward. Either I would become a pastor like my dad or a professional musician. I certainly grew up in the church and was blessed by having the best education anyone could have in that regard. I was surrounded by talented musicians who gave me the love of melodies and the written word. At at eighteen years old I was convinced that either one of those pursuits would be my own life's calling.

Little did I realize at the time that one chance encounter in a health club would change my life; God surely had a different plan for me, though it was somewhat strange how it unfolded.

Gateway College was a school that focused on theology and music, and many of my friends who went there had dreams of either becoming a pastor or a professional musician, just like me. In high school, most of my friends knew that because I was the preacher's kid I didn't smoke or drink. They enjoyed hanging out with me because I always liked to have fun and also because I could be their designated driver. Their parents felt the same way, and thought I was a good influence on their children. The truth is I loved sports way too much, which affected my grades for sure, and piano lessons were my nemesis. Regardless, I entered college hoping either theology or religion would be my calling.

One of the requirements of being a theology major was that every student was required to preach. Yes, actually prepare and deliver sermons to a live audience. We had to do this at small churches around the Greater St. Louis area, and I soon discovered it was not for me. I never felt comfortable and was always very nervous. Maybe it was because Dad was so good at it, and I just never felt good enough? I remember struggling to write words that I thought would be meaningful and that folks would want to hear.

But a funny thing happened during my college days. While I was starting to realize that being in the ministry was not a calling like it was for Dad, I realized something that I am continually grateful for to this day. Being a theology major taught me to really dig deep into the Bible and learn much more than I ever would have if I had gone in another direction. There are so many things I know today that I learned by reading and actually studying the Bible. Because I was music major, somehow the two disciplines gave me a spring in my step and the ability to think deeply about the world around me. Studying theology and music for so many years helped develop in me a type of daily discipline that really paid off in my future business years. I simply had to commit to a daily routine of study and practice in order to learn and advance in my college years.

When I reached a point in my twenties that I actually began to think seriously and critically about my future career, I had completed my first undergraduate degree at Gateway College. I knew I had to get serious about my future, and the best way for me to do that, I thought at the time, was to get another degree in business and finance. I came to realize two pivotal things while at Gateway College in St. Louis, Missouri. First, I didn't feel God's calling for me to become a minister and pastor of a church. Second, while I played the piano and baritone horn reasonably well and was a fairly good singer, I just wasn't at the level to do any of those occupations professionally. Luckily for me, after

I graduated from Gateway College, I immediately applied to Belmont University in Nashville, and the university accepted many of my class credits from Gateway College; I was able to complete my BBA degree in finance in just two years.

Right before I graduated, my Uncle Jim Hardwick, who happened to work for First American National Bank in Nashville, asked me if I wanted to consider getting a part-time job there. Uncle Jim had started his own business career after studying at Vanderbilt University and was the branch manager of the bank's Donelson branch, while another uncle of mine, Joe Carson, was the branch manager of the Harding Mall branch of First American National Bank.

There is nothing like having uncles in your life. I grew up being a sports fanatic, and both Uncle Jim and Uncle Joe were very good athletes. When we were boys, they would take Steve and me to baseball and football games all over Tennessee and beyond. Uncle Joe even took us on weekend road trips where we would watch the Cincinnati Reds play at the old Crosley Field in Cincinnati, Ohio. We visited so many Putt-Putt golf courses, where we would be thrilled to putt our way into the fire-breathing dragon's mouth or the pirate's wooden leg, earning endless accolades from our uncles and passersby. We were fiercely competitive for sure!

During my first year at Belmont University, Uncle Jim approached me with a novel idea. He had attended Vanderbilt University many years before, where he studied engineering. When the bank decided to enter into a joint venture partnership with Equitable Life Insurance Company to build a beautiful and modern high-rise office building in downtown Nashville, it decided to ask Uncle Jim to become the general manager of the partnership and oversee the new building project. "Mike, how would you like to work in the new thirty-one-story office tower in downtown Nashville?" he said. "We have a small but very nice men's health club that I know needs an evening and weekend manager." At twenty-one years old, I thought I had nothing to lose, plus I could put my newly found business knowledge to the test.

"Uncle Jim, that's fantastic," I said, knowing that I probably could ace that job since I had worked literally all of my young adult life and all through college to help pay for my tuition. "That sounds like a great idea! What do you think I would have to do in that job?"

"Mike, here's what they want you to do," Uncle Jim said. "The club is located on the roof of the building, there's an elevator that takes you to the top floor, and then you walk up some stairs to get to the roof. To be eligible to become a member, you have to maintain an office in the bank office tower, and most of the people who work there are professionals such as bankers, attorneys, and accountants. The club officially closes every day at 8:00 PM, but you will need to stay there until each and every member leaves, plus you have to make sure that the memberships are up-to-date and that the bills go out on time. One more thing, you will have to do some straightening up, too."

"Count me in, Uncle," I said.

So, now I had a job of real status and responsibility, or so I thought. The truth was that I was really just a glorified janitor, but working an extra thirty to forty hours each week and earning some serious money was worth it in my book.

It was 8:40 PM on a hot Wednesday night in the summer of 1975, obviously past closing time, and I was just about to finish up my work when I noticed that one man was still left in the club. Not just any man. He was Mr. T. Scott Fillebrown, the distinguished president of First American National Bank, which had become the largest bank in the state of Tennessee at the time. I decided to go about my business and let him finish his shower. I continued to sit at my desk and get some paperwork done. (My desk faced the side wall of the men's locker room, so I could see who was coming and going but not much else, fortunately.)

Mr. Fillebrown had a towel wrapped around him as he walked out of the shower room and into the men's locker room, then walked across the locker room and sat on the wooden bench facing his locker.

I was somewhat intimated by Mr. Fillebrown, since he was much older and, of course, the president of the bank. When talking with distinguished businesspeople like Mr. Fillebrown, at times I could hardly get my words out, which was very unusual for me even as a young man. "Ugh, ugh, Mr. Fillebrown, how can I help you," I muttered as I tried my best not to look at him anywhere else except his face.

"Hardwick, I heard you are about to graduate and need a job," he said.

"Yes, sir, that is true," I told him, still trying to avoid his half-naked body! "Well, Hardwick, have you got a full-time job yet?"

"No, sir, I don't as of yet, but I am interviewing at P&G, Cintas Corp., and a few other companies."

"Hardwick, you didn't mention the bank! Why wouldn't you interview here at First American, since both of your uncles work here?" he said.

"Well, sir, I thought that if I did, it would break some kind of nepotism rules, and I didn't want to do that," I told him, though I was hoping he would prove me wrong.

Sure enough, right after I said that, he smiled and said, "Son, your uncles are two of our best!"

As I turned around in my chair to talk to him, I almost had a heart attack! There he was, Mr. Fillebrown, the president of the largest bank in Tennessee, standing just twenty feet away from me in nothing but a towel and beet red from the hot steam shower he had just finished taking. He was still sweating profusely, so I nervously asked him if he wanted to sit down.

Then things went from bad to worst. His towel, which I was hoping would never reveal what was underneath, slipped off of his body very unexpectedly. This was my worst nightmare ever! First he had a towel wrapped around him during our conversation, and now he was standing right across the room from me buck naked! "Where's the phone, Hardwick, I need to make a call." I nervously handed him the phone hoping the line would reach far enough, and this time I did not look anywhere on that man's person except for the whites of his eyes. "George, this is Scott," he said. "I'm at the health club with Hardwick, this young man who works here and who would like to interview for a job. What time can he come in and meet with you tomorrow?"

It turns out that the *George* he was talking to was George Miller, the human resources director for the bank. "So, Hardwick," he turned to me and said, "Would 4:00 PM tomorrow work for you to come in for an interview?"

Wow, would 4:00 PM work for *me*? I couldn't believe what I was hearing, but I was more than happy to oblige. "Thank you, sir, for giving me this opportunity," I said. "You don't know how much this means to me."

"Hardwick, you are a fine young man, and you will be a great addition to our team."

Suddenly I forgot that I was talking to the naked president of the largest bank in Tennessee!

The next day I woke up bright and early, the sun shining through my bedroom window, which is always a good sign. I hopped out of bed, took a hot shower and dressed in my best suit; I just couldn't wait to get my day started. The day seemed to drag on and last forever, but finally 4:00 PM rolled around, and I was ready for my big interview with Mr. Miller. His office was on the third floor. I made my way through the lobby and onto the elevator of the First American Center building.

This just may be what God has planned for me, I thought to myself, as the elevator was almost at the third floor. As I walked toward Mr. Miller's office, I clearly knew that the ministry or the orchestra wasn't in my future, but *banking*? Following in the footsteps of my uncles? That had never really entered my mind, yet here I was preparing to interview at the very same bank where Uncle Jim and Uncle Joe had both built great careers.

"Come right in, Hardwick, and take a seat; I'll be right with you," Mr. Miller said. I was nervous for sure, but had my game face on and was ready for my future—whatever that was. As his assistant led me into his office, which was rather small but still had that feel of importance, I sat down in front of Mr. Miller's desk. After a few minutes of the requisite chitchat, he said, "So, Hardwick, when can you start?"

"What do you mean, sir," I said to him, not believing what I was hearing.

"I mean when can you start working at the bank?" Was he kidding? Did he know that I hadn't graduated from Belmont yet? "Hardwick, here's the deal. If Scott wants to hire you; you're hired!"

"That's great, Mr. Miller, but might I ask you what I will be doing?"

"Hardwick, I'm going to put you in our management training program. It's about eighteen months long, and you will get exposure to all of our six operating divisions and will have a chance to train in all of those departments." I had a few friends who went through that program, and they all said it was terrific, so I was really excited about his proposition.

This was my big moment! The plans for my future were now becoming crystal clear. "Mr. Miller, I would be honored to work at the bank, but would you mind telling me what the pay is?"

"Son, the starting pay for the program is $7.00 an hour." You could have heard a pin drop. Frankly I was stunned at that low figure, and surely thought I was worth more than that.

"Mr. Miller that is a bit disappointing to me because I heard there was a pay range of between $7.00 and $8.50 for the position," I said to him, very surprised that I was able to muster the courage to ask him such a bold question.

"Well, Hardwick, what do you think you are worth?" he asked me.

"Sir, I have been told that you have to have a graduate degree to start at the $8.50 per hour, which I don't have. I would say I am worth at least $7.75 or $8.00," I replied.

"Okay, Hardwick, we will start you out at $8.00."

I was thrilled, I really was, but I couldn't help asking him just one more question. "Mr. Miller, can I ask you something?"

"Sure, son, what is it?"

"Well, if I would have asked you for the entire $8.50 an hour, would I have still gotten the job?"

"Hardwick, you should have asked me that in the first place. Of course you would."

I excitedly shook Mr. Miller's hand and left his office knowing that I was going to become a banker. Where that path would take me I didn't know yet, but I was on my way. As a boy I was almost positive I would follow in my father's footsteps. As a young man, I was following my own calling. God had a different plan for me. Though my early education focused on music and theology, my business studies helped me secure my future.

Now I was going to become a banker, a profession where generally your success is measured by how much money you make. Period!

But in the back of my mind, and because of how I had been taught all of my young life to that point, I knew that my success would be determined by a higher order. Success for me was, "Having enough to do what God has called you to do."

I have often thought that my coincidental encounter with Mr. Fillebrown at the health club might not have been such an accident after all. For it was there that I met a man just a few short years later who would precipitate the next chapter in my business career. I would never have dreamed of asking him for a job. But he saw something in me, and I am sure it was because he could sense that I had my own calling and had what it took to become a banker.

My glorified janitor days were over.

CHAPTER 5

How Dick Freeman
Launched My Career

Success always demands a greater effort.—Winston Churchill

Things were going very well for me at First American National Bank (FANB). I started my new career fresh out of Belmont University in the bank's management training program and was so blessed to be part of such a dynamic company, one that I knew would be going places. At twenty-four years old, I felt, for the first time in my life, that working in the business field was the right career choice. My only trepidation was that I hoped when I would see Mr. Fillebrown he wouldn't notice the flush on my face or the awkward pause in my speech.

The first week on the job was exhilarating. I remember so vividly walking into the bank wearing my new dark blue business suit, complete with a white starched shirt and red tie and shiny black wing-tip shoes, feeling like I had now finally arrived. After a few days at work, I quickly began to realize that just because I had completed my college degree, I had little to no real specific banking training, and it was obvious that I still had so much to learn. Uncle Jim and Uncle Joe were very thrilled that I was part of the First American team, and Dad—though I am sure would probably have preferred me following in his footsteps and becoming a minister—still was extremely proud and happy that I made the right choice for me.

After having worked in the management training program for about nine months, I got a call one morning from a good friend, Sam Bartholomew. Sam was a relatively young man who was being groomed to possibly become the next president of the bank and was someone I had gotten to know quite well during my time working in the bank's health club over the previous two years. Recruited by Coach Paul Dietzel to play college football at the United States Military Academy, Sam became captain of the first Army team to play the University of Tennessee Volunteers in Neyland Stadium in 1965. At West Point, he was cadet captain, battalion commander, and assistant football coach in 1966. Obviously, Sam was a very athletic man, and we had enjoyed many battles on the racquetball court with him winning some, but me usually beating him. I was thrilled that Sam called me into his office one day to offer to me what he described as a "great opportunity."

As he revealed when he was explaining the bank's history, about two years prior they had acquired the largest nondepository mortgage banking firm in Tennessee at the time, an independently owned statewide mortgage bank known as Guaranty Mortgage Company (GMC). Shortly after acquiring GMC, the bank found that a large number of commercial real estate loans made by GMC in prior years were simply going bad. What that means is that the borrower failed to make timely payments and/or the loans were made unwisely or imprudently. The volume of bad loans was significant enough that the board of directors of FANB had made the decision to create a new division within the bank to focus solely on working out the large portfolio of bad loans, and they had named Sam to head up that effort. The new division was called the Special Assets Division. Sam was told that he could select four to five young men within the bank to move into this newly formed group to work with him in dealing with these problem loans.

After talking it through with Sam that morning, I told him that I very much appreciated his offer, but didn't really feel that I wanted to accept it due to my desire to stay focused early in my career on becoming a commercial banker, instead of moving into the real estate side of banking. He requested that I take a day to think it over and then let him know. That evening when I got home from work, the first person I called was Uncle Jim. I had great respect for him and trusted his thinking, so I talked through the opportunity with him at length. I'll never forget what he told me. He said, "Mike, you would be a fool to not accept that opportunity! You would be working with a small and select team of guys on possibly the most important issues for the bank, and you would be personally reporting to the FANB board of directors every couple of weeks on the progress of your efforts. Mike, having that type of actual face time with some of the real leaders in the city would be invaluable for your future."

I thanked Uncle Jim for his sage advice and called Sam back the following day and accepted his offer.

Wow, was Uncle Jim ever right! Over the next couple of years, our small team was able to resolve many of the problem loans, and we saved the bank millions of dollars in losses that would have otherwise hit it hard on the bottom line. And my uncle was so right about some other things, too. Soon after I took the job, I became well known on a first name basis by some of the city's best-known lawyers, accountants, and businessmen who sat on the FANB board.

Fellows like Mr. John C. Tune, a Nashville attorney, civic leader, longtime aviation enthusiast, and one of the principal developers of the modern aviation authority concept. He was also a former chairman of the Metropolitan Nashville Airport Authority. Planning for the construction of a new airport began in 1965 under Nashville's former Department of Aviation as a reliever airport designed to provide additional capacity at Nashville International Airport (Berry Field). This new airport was named the John C. Tune Airport in recognition of Mr. Tune's many valuable contributions to the city of Nashville.

Also, another FANB director was Mr. Nelson C. Andrews, who was yet another Nashville business icon who played a decisive role in the creation of Vanderbilt's Children's Hospital, Leadership Nashville, and the Nashville Alliance for Public Education, as well as the Better

Business Bureau of Nashville/Middle Tennessee, among other local institutions. As chairman of the Tennessee Board of Education in the 1980s and 1990s, he shepherded the creation of a new funding mechanism for the state's public schools. At the time of his passing, he was chairman of the Tennessee Tax Structure Study Commission. Mr. Andrews was an extremely kind and generous gentleman who invested much time in me personally.

To this day, many of the board of directors of First American National Bank from those early days are still friends of mine, and have helped me in so many ways over my forty-year business career.

These were some of the happiest days of my life. Working at the bank gave me so much exposure and experience, but, after working there for nearly five years, I found myself a bit restless and ready for a new challenge and opportunity. I loved working at the bank, and had made excellent progress, having been named assistant vice president at the age of twenty-seven, which I later found was one of the youngest in the history of the bank. I really thought I would stay there forever, but after having been passed over for a promotion, which in my heart I felt I deserved, I became not just restless but truly discontented. I should add that in later years I realized that I was not ready for the promotion opportunity and would have no doubt failed, thus potentially derailing my career. Sometimes, as Garth Brooks's song "Unanswered Prayers" says, "Sometimes I thank God for unanswered prayers."

During my first year at the bank, I began working on an MBA degree at the University of Tennessee in Nashville (UTN) on a part-time basis a couple of evenings during the week. One of my classes at UTN was a graduate-level economics class taught by a local businessman by the name of Ken Elrod, who was heading up a company known as the J. C. Bradford Properties Company. This company was owned by J. C. Bradford Company, which was reputedly the largest investment banking firm headquartered in the South at the time. Ken Elrod was an exceptionally bright fellow, having been a University of Tennessee graduate with an MBA degree in finance and economics; we became fast friends.

Over the semester while I was enrolled in that class, I shared some of my feelings with Ken Elrod, seeking his advice, and to my surprise and delight, he offered me a new opportunity to become a vice president with J. C. Bradford Properties. As we talked the offer through, I learned that I would be able to double my annual income immediately and move to one of the most respected financial companies in the South. I felt possibly for the first time the entrepreneurial bug bite, and though I wasn't sure how that would play itself out, I was ready to accept a change.

Within just a few short weeks, I made the decision to leave FANB and move one block down the street to the corner of Fourth Avenue and Church Street, where J. C. Bradford Properties had its headquarters. On my very first day there, I was invited to meet with the big boss, Mr. J. C. Bradford Sr. in his impressive office on the top floor. Imagine, here I was just a young fellow in my late twenties, and I was being asked to meet with a business legend! Mr. Bradford had started his namesake company in the depths of the years of the Great Depression, and he had built it into one of the most successful companies in the history of Nashville. Mr. Bradford was a very special man who seemed to truly care about his employees. He made a habit of spending a few minutes with most new hires on their first day at work whenever possible. I could have never imagined at the time that his words would become part of my own blueprint for a corporate culture twenty years later.

While I was sitting in his office, surrounded by photos of his family and many of the movers and shakers in Nashville, he made a comment to me that I found very interesting. It was so compelling, in fact, that I never forgot it, and I have even used it many times over the four decades of my own career. He told me that at Bradford they operated under what he called the broomsweeper theory. His theory simply meant that whenever anyone at Bradford needed help with his or her particular job, other employees were expected to take a few minutes to try and offer the person help when at all possible.

He gave me this example of the broomsweeper theory at work: "Mr. Hardwick, if you are in a meeting with a client, and I happen to walk by and notice his or her coffee cup needs to be refilled, then I will take a moment to bring your client a fresh cup of coffee. And if you are walking past the receptionist and the phones are ringing faster than she might be able to keep up, will you be willing to stop for a few minutes to help her catch up?"

This was my answer to Mr. Bradford's question? If he, the founder and owner of one of the top investment banking firms in the country, was willing to help me, then how could I do otherwise? "Of course, Mr. Bradford," I said. "I love the concept of the broomsweeper theory, and you can count on me to help when I can. I'm impressed that other people actually want to help each other out, no matter what their job description or position within the company. This is a great concept to instill into each employee, and I would be proud to be part of that kind of caring team," I said.

I was literally spellbound.

After I left the meeting, I was truly inspired. For the next couple of years, I worked hard learning about the real estate development business, playing a role in the land acquisition and building of approximately thirty-plus strip shopping centers across Tennessee, North Carolina, South Carolina, and Georgia. To this day, when I am driving down interstate highways in these states, I often take a little time to exit and drive by one of these shopping centers just to see how the properties look, even though they are all much older properties now. It always brings me a feeling of pride to know that at such a young age I was able to participate in these exciting investment ventures and learn so much at the same time.

After a couple of years working at J. C. Bradford Properties, I received a telephone call one day from Mr. Dick Freeman, who my wife was working for at the time. He invited me to lunch the following day, and at that lunch meeting I began to get the entrepreneurial itch again. Mr. Freeman was one of the more successful real estate businesspeople in the entire South, having built with his father and brothers several different and highly successful real estate companies.

I was still working at J. C. Bradford Properties and felt just slightly uncomfortable talking to Mr. Freeman. I was a very loyal person, and didn't realize at the time that most people have an average of seven or more jobs in their lifetime. I thought that by speaking with Mr. Freeman, I would somehow not be a loyal Bradford employee. On the other hand, the one thing I learned from all of my sales experience was that you never know what doors will open for you if you don't take a risk and try. So I made my way up to Mr. Freeman's office, which was on the opposite corner at Fourth Avenue and Church Street in the Third National Bank Building, and was prepared to see if there might be a job opportunity that would fit my youthful energy and financial experience.

As I walked into his office Mr. Freeman said, "Mike, it's a pleasure to meet with you. Having gotten to know you and your wonderful family over the past couple of years or so, I am so glad you agreed to meet with me."

"Mr. Freeman, it is my honor," I said, thinking to myself that this just might be another big break I had really been hoping would happen.

He continued, "I am starting this new real estate venture. It is a project where we take existing apartment buildings, go through the legal process of turning them into condominiums, and then sell them to the public. Mike, it has the potential to be a really big business, and it takes someone who has a great personality, is highly organized, and has leadership qualities and also sales ability to be successful. I think you would be perfect for the job."

He had already successfully converted a couple of properties and was now interested in actually building a business around that concept. After talking with me about the business idea, he asked me if I would be interested in helping him by taking on the role as president of his new enterprise.

Needless to say, I was ecstatic! This was something that intrigued me to no end and would give me the chance to once again double my income. If I was really successful, I could even triple or quadruple it, plus I would essentially be my own boss. I would also have the opportunity to travel, which I have always loved, and, at the same time, grow a business based on my own talents and experience.

I recall asking him, "Why me? Mr. Freeman, I don't know anything about the condo conversion business, and frankly I'm not sure I could even spell the word condominium."

"Mike," he said enthusiastically, "you are young, energetic, well-educated, have a solid financial background from your banking training, you meet people easily, and you have a winning personality." His words made me feel very much empowered and quite important! Then, he told me, "Mike, the primary reason that I know you will be successful is that I know you want to learn and will listen to my advice. If I am correct, then I can teach you so you can learn the business."

Well, after about a nanosecond of thinking about his offer and praying about this new opportunity, I decided to go for it. "Mr. Freeman, I would be thrilled to work for you, and I want to thank you for believing in me and giving me this chance to start a new career," I said.

That had to be one of the very best business decisions I have ever made. That's because Mr. Freeman, or Dick, as he asked me to call him, over the ensuing twenty-five years became one of the two real meaningful mentors in my life. He proved to be one of the most generous businessmen I have ever had the privilege of knowing. He was not only very fair with me in terms of the compensation he paid me over the following years of work, but he also was extremely interested in me as a person. He cared so much for me and my family, and he invested significant amounts of time in training me, not only in the condo conversion business, but even more so in how to build a successful company. He taught me so much about business in general and instilled in me a confidence and belief that I could actually build a company from the ground up.

To say we enjoyed enormous success in that business over the next six to seven years would truly be an understatement. With the direction and mentorship of Dick and the commitment and hard work of many wonderful employees, we were successful in building SEC Realty Corporation into one of the most successful and profitable condo conversion companies in America. As a side note, me being a college football enthusiast and particularly fond of the Southeastern Conference, or SEC, as it has been referred to for many years, the name of our condo conversion company was easy to choose. For our purposes, the term SEC stood for Southeastern Conversion Corporation, but to me it was always a double entendre.

Who knew that over the seven or so short years I worked for Mr. Freeman, his guidance and mentorship would dramatically change my life forever?

Magnolia Oaks was a 109-unit apartment building located in the coastland near Pascagoula, Mississippi, in a very small community known as Gautier, Mississippi. I took a flight every Monday morning from Nashville to Gulfport, Mississippi, and then rented a car to take me from the Gulfport airport to Gautier, which was about forty miles away. We didn't have GPS back then, so I had to look on a map to see exactly where I was going. I was having some trouble finding the place. So, I drove to the next gas station I could find. "Excuse me, sir, I'm trying to find this town, and I was wondering if you could help me find it on the map," I said. I obviously was mispronouncing the word Gautier, as he quickly corrected my pronunciation. "Son, I don't know the town you just mentioned, but there is a place called, 'Gautier,' and it is pronounced 'Goshay,' which is a Cajun term, so I guess that's the place you are trying to find. Here's where it is, and you are only about twenty miles away." I quickly realized that even as a southerner myself, folks in this part of the country spoke a little differently than we do in Tennessee!

I thanked the service man, got back in my rental car and finally made it to my destination. I had rented an apartment there, and planned to stay in Mississippi from Monday through Friday every week and then make my way back to Nashville for the weekends. One of my first objectives was to finalize my business plan and then get started putting it into place. Mr. Freeman gave me tons of good advice and was there for me if I needed his help and guidance. But I was kind of headstrong at the time, and I daresay a little cocky, and thought that I could make this work on my own terms. Failure, as always, was not an option.

During the early 1980s, the idea of turning apartments into condominiums was a relatively novel one for rural and smaller towns. The concept was to give folks the dream of homeownership at an affordable price. Rather than have to throw away their hard-earned money on rent, people would now be able to build a nest egg and know that the money they earned was going into an investment for their family's future. For those folks who owned businesses in town, it was another way for them to create wealth by owning the condos and then reselling them at a later time for a higher price. The condos varied in size and price. I would say that they averaged about twelve hundred square feet, and cost about $40,000 each. Also, in those days there were significant tax advantages to owning investment real estate.

Since I knew virtually no one in Gautier, my plan was to go door-to-door and essentially cold call on all of the business owners in town. This came very naturally to me since I learned how to do this by selling those Krispy Kreme doughnuts and hot lunches to raise money for our church when I was just a boy. Throughout my youth, I had the satisfaction of knowing that all of my hard work truly paid off, and now those same skills would give me the financial security I had always dreamed about—that is, if I was successful.

Those first few weeks were absolutely exhilarating. I got up every morning with a spring in my step, anxious to meet the rental tenants of Magnolia Oaks and the businesspeople of Pascagoula, Gulfport, and, of course, Gautier, and present them with this unique opportunity. Mr. Freeman was also very pleased with my progress and plan of attack. Here's what I would say when I went from business to business trying to cultivate potential investors: "My name is Mike Hardwick, and I'm so pleased to meet you and have the good fortune to present you with this once-in-a-lifetime business opportunity. I work for Mr. Dick Freeman in Nashville, and he is a very well-known and respected real estate developer in Middle Tennessee. We have purchased Magnolia Oaks Apartments and are going to convert each one into a condominium. For a small investment of up to $40,000, you can purchase one or more of these units, depending on the size, and we estimate that in five years or so that initial investment could be up to at least $50,000 per unit. I know you will be most pleased with being part of such an innovative and rewarding program like this."

Then, after my initial pitch, I would give them a packet with all of the financial details of the deal, a rendering of the condominiums and background information on Mr. Freeman and his real estate record. Nine times out of ten, the folks in town bought into the idea and committed to purchasing not only one unit, but two or three units. To my surprise, in just ninety days we actually sold and closed all of the 109 units. We were so successful that we had to use the clubhouse to conduct our closings en masse. It was so busy that I had to hire my first employee, Opal Haub, to help me with all of the paperwork and keep track of the sales. Our attorney, Steve Baker with Dearborn and Ewing Law Firm in Nashville, even had to fly down to help us close all of the sales over a three- or four-day period of time. (I actually did every single job on this first conversion from handling the remodeling of the property, to selling all the units, to taking each of the loan applications, underwriting each file, and handling all of the closing process.) We kept chopping wood, as I like to say, and there was no sign of us ever slowing down. By the way, I first heard that phrase during a sideline interview at a football game when the coach motivated his players by telling them to keep chopping wood. Jack Del Rio, the former NFL player and now head coach of the Oakland Raiders, coined the phrase when he was the head coach of the Jacksonville Jaguars. He initiated it during that 2003 season, and it was intended to indicate how the team would slowly whittle away the huge obstacles that lay in front of them. Del Rio placed a wooden stump and ax in the Jaguars' locker room as a symbol of that theme and a constant reminder of his "keep chopping wood" rallying cry. I've used that wonderful motivational tool with my own team ever since. By that, I simply mean you oftentimes have to intentionally persevere and push through when things become more difficult or seem too daunting. We talk often about how important it is to have a never-quit, never-give-up attitude, and how critical it is simply to keep doing the right activities every day, not just now and then. Life at various times hits you hard, both personally and professionally. I cannot overstate the importance of keeping a mind-set of stability, determined focus, and a deciding to never giving up or giving in! In other words, keep chopping wood!

Those were some of the best years of my life. I was still a young buck, and I must say, earning some big bucks, too. In the six years that I worked for Mr. Freeman, I was more successful than I could have ever dreamed. I was earning well over six figures, which at the time was considered extremely unusual for a young person in his or her late twenties to early thirties, and I was literally on top of the world. Mr. Freeman was happy with my performance too, and year after year he would give me stellar reviews and some very impactful business advice as well as words of wisdom that I remember and cherish to this day. Some of those memorable gems included this prophetic metaphor: "I don't want any cheese, I just want out of the trap." What he meant by that was the "trap" of his own excessive debt, which eventually caused him to go into bankruptcy. He would also frequently tell me and all of his employees, "The most important words in real estate are timing, timing, timing." This was a little contradictory to the usual answer of, location, location, location, but, as Mr. Freeman correctly taught me, the best location in the world will not allow you to make much money if you have purchased it at the wrong time, where you will be overpaying for sure!

During that time, I could have never predicted that those words would come back to haunt me and take a different and catastrophic turn for the worst. After many years of unbridled success, an event that none of us could have ever predicted drove us out of business in a span of approximately eighteen months.

With one stroke of a presidential pen, my life would take a turn that no one, let alone me, would have ever imagined. President Ronald Reagan signed into law the "Tax Reform Act of 1986," and its effects began to take hold of businesses like ours with draconian consequences.

CHAPTER 6

I Had It All; I Lost It All:
The Terrible Roller Coaster of Depression

If opportunity doesn't knock, build a door.—Milton Berle

The Tax Reform Act of 1986 was signed into law by President Ronald Reagan, and enacted by the Ninety-Ninth Congress on October 22, 1986. It was introduced in the US House of Representatives as HR 3838 by Dan Rostenkowski (D-IL), head of the powerful House Ways and Means Committee. It was passed in the House on December 17, 1985, passed in the Senate on June 24, 1986, and then it went to the Joint Conference Committee on September 18, and was agreed to by the House on September 25 and by the Senate on September 27. The goal of the legislation was to simplify the tax code, expand the tax base, and totally eliminate many tax shelters and other loopholes that businesses have used for years. It was also designed to increase revenue by increasing taxes on corporations and capital gains, among others, and it also reduced the number of deductions and tax brackets for individuals as well.

While it was certainly a surprise coming from Republican President Ronald Reagan, nonetheless, it sounded like a good idea, right? Well, for Dick Freeman, all of us who worked for him, our commercial real estate investment industry, and the savings and loan industry too, it was literally the beginning of the end.

I was thirty-five years old at the time and married with two young daughters—Shayna and Megan—at home. I was on top of the world.

While I didn't have the crazy kind of financial success that Bill Gates had, I was blessed to enjoy a solid and methodical success that I was so proud to have achieved throughout my entire business career, though still relatively short at the time. I was the youngest vice president at First American National Bank, and I had the good fortune of working for J. C. Bradford Properties Inc., a division of the largest investment banking firm headquartered in the Southeast, where I quickly learned even more about real estate lending and property development. Success was very important to me, and every year my hard work paid off with added responsibilities and more income. After nearly twelve years of hard work, I could honestly say that I was now at the top of my game working for my mentor, Dick Freeman, and his condo conversion company. And I felt really great about making a yearly salary and bonus that was well over $250,000. For a couple of years I actually earned closer to $500,000, which, considering the value of money at the time, was an amazing income, especially for such a young guy. And I needed it too. I had a growing family to feed, friends and relatives who I wanted to help, my church, which I always wanted to support financially, and children whose future I was determined to secure, so making a good living was always one of my top priorities.

Then, as the Tax Reform Act began to be implemented from 1986 to 1987, many of the tax incentives for the folks who owned commercial or residential real estate investments—some of whom were passive investors, those who got together to invest in real estate—were wiped out. Many of these real estate holdings were purchased based on their inherent profitability on paper, and which received significant tax benefits that also provided enormous savings on other earned income. Many of these real estate investments at times mainly depended upon those tax savings as the primary incentive for making the investment rather than just the actual future value of the real estate properties. With the Tax Reform Act of 1986 fully implemented, any financial losses from these investments could now not be deducted from the investor's gross income, and as a result, little by little the real estate industry was decimated. This became especially true due to the fact that this tax act was made retroactive. Clearly, the boom of the 1980s was coming to a tragic and painful end for not only tens of thousands of real estate investors, but for me and my great friend and mentor Dick Freeman.

This was literally the first time in my life that I had a major setback, and boy was it a doozey!

It was in early to mid-1987 when Mr. Freeman and I sat down to assess the damage. While I had seen the handwriting on the wall, I was, nevertheless, in a state of shock when he said, "Mike, we are in deep trouble. I mean serious trouble." As Mr. Freeman told me, my heart sank in my chest. "All of our holdings are now worth little to nothing, having lost tremendous value due to much of the income tax benefits being retroactively taken away. Mike, I'm going to have to declare bankruptcy and lay off all of our employees."

"Mr. Freeman isn't there anything left for us to salvage, or any strategy we should consider to save our business from total collapse," I asked him, knowing full well that the good times in the real estate industry were over. "Mike, I'm sorry to say this, but the Tax Reform Act has put us out of business."

As the days dragged on, I realized more and more just what happened to us and to all of the other companies that were involved in investment residential and commercial real estate at the time. Everyone, including the savings and loan associations, as well as many major insurance companies and banks that invested heavily in these types of tax-advantaged investments, were negatively affected by this legislation. In fact, the FDIC reported that 1,043 thrifts failed or were otherwise resolved from 1986 to 1995, representing assets of $519 billion. The failure of those savings and loan associations, as well as the failure of many of the large commercial banks at the time, led to the crisis we were now experiencing. Ultimately, if there were fewer places for customers to obtain mortgages, no tax incentives for large investors, retroactive penalties for companies that took advantage of the previous tax shelters and loopholes, and companies like ours that were now worth nothing on paper, it was a complete disaster for the real estate industry and a devastating blow for countless real estate businesspeople, such as me and Dick Freeman.

This was our industry's perfect storm, and Mr. Freeman and I were stuck at sea with no food, water, or lifeboats to save us.

As those long and emotionally draining days went by painfully slowly, I had to come to grips with the grim tasks ahead. With having to lay off employees, watching a man I admired and loved go through a devastating loss, having to tell my family that we were nearly bankrupt, and wondering if I even had a future ahead of me, these were all unfamiliar and uncomfortable feelings that I was totally unprepared to handle. Still, I had a job to do, and so I went through the gut-wrenching steps of telling some of the best and brightest people who worked for us that they no longer had jobs. Our eight-thousand-square-foot main office felt like a morgue, with only three employees left out of the many we had just a few weeks before. I felt as if I had had a mental lobotomy, literally walking from empty office to empty office asking myself what went wrong. What could I have done to make things better? How could I have not known what this legislation was going to do to our business? How could I have let down my family, my church, and my employees?

As the days, then weeks, then months went painfully by, I found myself in a mental fugue. Instead of waking up every morning feeling energized and motivated as I had felt all of my life, I found it difficult to muster up the energy to just get out of bed most mornings. My normally clean-shaven face was now full of stubble, and my eyes were sunken deep, something even I noticed when I finally did have the energy to get out of bed and look into the mirror. My thoughts were racing in my head, mostly trying to come to grips with my business failure and fleeting feelings of my self-worth. I am sure many people have felt the very same way, tying their personal identities and feelings of value strictly to what they did or did not do for a living. For me, these two were inextricably entwined. Now that I had no income and no job, I truly believed that my life was over in terms of ever being able to build a business and provide well for my family.

Over the next eight to ten months or so, it was obvious to many that I was experiencing clinical depression, and I needed help. I couldn't deal with it alone and had no idea what to do to change the course of my negative thinking. One day Dad came over to the house and was concerned about what he could clearly see was a person in need of a pastor. "Son, you will get out of this, I promise you," he said. "Mom and I are here with you, and we will help you and, though we don't have all of the answers, we believe in you and love you." Those words were so comforting to me at the time, but as soon as Dad left, I felt that deep sense of dread and uselessness return.

According to the Mayo Clinic, to be diagnosed with clinical depression you must meet the symptom criteria for the disorder and have five or more of the symptoms listed in the Diagnostic and Statistical Manual of Mental Disorders (DSM) which is published by the American Psychiatric Association. Some of them include: depressed mood, reduced interest or feeling no pleasure in all or most activities, significant weight loss or gain, insomnia, restlessness or slowed behavior, fatigue or loss of energy, feelings of worthlessness, trouble making decisions, and recurring thoughts of suicide. While thankfully I never had any thoughts of suicide or ever turned to medication for help, I easily had five of these symptoms and was officially clinically depressed. (I later learned that depression is a common mental disorder that affects more than 14.8 million American adults from all walks of life, or about 6.7 percent of the population; however, it can at times be treated successfully by medication and counseling.)

Nashville, back then, was a relatively small to midsized city, and like most similar towns in this great nation of ours, people talk. And talk they did. Soon, it was widely known in the circles in which I ran that, "Mike Hardwick was down in the dumps," or "Mike Hardwick lost all of his money," but no matter what people thought or said, I was the one most aware that I needed some sort of divine intervention. What I didn't know at the time was that it would come in the form of a rather large, chain-smoking businessman with a bright red ketchup stain on his tie. Meet my muse, Mike Ballard.

"Hey, Mike, this is Ballard calling, and I want to get together with you for lunch. Call me back soon, buddy." The last thing I wanted to do is go out to lunch with anybody, but for some unknown reason on this particular day, I thought meeting Mike might actually help cheer me up. My friend Mike Ballard is a great guy. By that I mean not only is he smart, but he is also a very interesting fellow to just talk to and spend time with. Besides that, we had so much in common, especially our love of sports and our obsession with football. Ballard grew up in Wisconsin and is a big Green Bay Packers fan. I grew up watching Vince Lombardi lead Bart Starr, Paul Hornung, and the Packers to many NFL championships, so I guess it is safe to say that I was as much of a cheesehead as Ballard.

We decided to go to a restaurant in town called Pargos, which was in Brentwood, Tennessee, a suburb of Nashville. I met him about 3:30 PM, and we were among the only people eating there at the time. When I first laid my eyes on Mike, he made me smile. He has what I would describe as a puppy dog face, with very thick eyebrows and droopy eyes, and he is as nice and fun a man as anyone could ever know. For years, most times when we would get together, he would tell a great joke that got things off to a stellar start.

Ballard was wearing a typical investment banker's blue pinstripe suit with a vest, though his vest had a couple of buttons missing, his white shirt hanging out of his pants, and a very obvious stain on his tie that I assumed he got as he nibbled on some french fries right before I arrived. Ballard had his own string of business successes and failures, too, having made a ton of money as an investment banker, losing it all like me, then rebuilding his career and regaining everything he lost and more.

He was smoking like a chimney throughout our lunch, something that usually bothers me much, but as we were sipping our sweet tea, the smoke from his cigarettes seemed to dissipate as we were engrossed in conversation about everything from the market to our families. Then out of the blue he looked at me with his soulful eyes and said, "Mike, tell me what's goin' on." Well, that was all I needed to hear. For the next hour or more, I was dumping on him all of the bad stuff that happened to me and what a terrible person I thought I was because of the failure of our business and my financial problems. He listened intently, let me finish my "pity party," and then said something that at the time I didn't know would impact me in such a profound way. He leaned forward with his arms folded at the edge of the table, looked me dead square in the eye, and said, "Hardwick, you want me to tell you what your problem is? Mike, you've lost your faith in God!"

I was speechless. I thought, *Who are you, Ballard, you overweight, chain-smoking turkey, to be telling me—a preacher's kid who never missed a church service in his life—that I've lost my faith in God? Who are you to be telling* me?"

That was the self-righteous thought that ran through my mind in a nanosecond! Needless to say, this didn't sit well with me at all, but I simply still had too much pride to ever say that directly to Mike. I just responded with a comment like, "Mike, I hope not. Be sure to keep me in your prayers!"

I left the lunch feeling even worse than I did when I arrived, and though I was miffed at Mike for saying what he said, I did recognize at some level that he was just trying to help me, though at the time I didn't appreciate his comment, for sure. Thankfully, Mike was a great friend, and he had earned the right to say something like that to me without me getting too frustrated and really angry with him.

Despite having Dad as my pastor, family and friends who stayed close to me, and trying my best to keep it all together, I couldn't shake my feelings of failure and unworthiness. That night, like most every night, I couldn't sleep and thought that by reading the newspaper it might take my mind off my feelings of self-loathing and despair. It was well after midnight, and the house was quiet as a church mouse, so I could hear the rustle of the pages as I turned one then the next trying to read some of the local stories.

As I turned the last page to read the final story, I realized I had not even remembered the last one I read. It was as if my mind was a colander, with all of the water running right through the holes. I couldn't connect at all to what I was reading, and, frustrated, I decided to call it a night. Just then I happened to notice the Bible lying on our coffee table, and I decided to pick it up and read through a few passages. But the same thing happened to me again. The words were just not making any sense. I became so frustrated that I put it down and just started to pray silently. I decided to repeat the prayers of petition, which are also referred to as supplication. These are requests made to God that ask for whatever needs concern us and also to give us God's gifts and resources so that we can fulfill His purposes. So I silently said to myself over and over, *Thank you for this day, God, but Lord I need your help. I think I may have lost my faith, but how could I have lost my faith in you? I'm doing all the right things, but I am having trouble. Please Lord, show me the way.*

As I kept repeating my prayers, it suddenly dawned on me. Like a lightning bolt in fact. At that very moment the floodgates seemed to open, and I realized that Ballard was right after all! I *did* lose my faith in God, and it took having many months of deep and very real depression to make me realize that God used my friend Mike Ballard to change the course of my life. He told me the truth, and it would be the truth that would set me free.

I soon realized that I could live without a great job; I could live without making a lot of money, but I simply could not live a meaningful life without the Lord. I had slowly grown accustomed to having enormous business success and making a lot of money. I had subconsciously thought it was all me that had created this tremendous success, and now that my business and income were both gone, I must be gone also! It was at that moment that I recalled Philippians 4:13, which said, "I can do all things through the Lord who strengthens me."

Over the next few months I continued to renew my faith in God and slowly but surely gained my energy and optimism back. The sun was shining brighter; I could feel the weight of my depression lifting, and I was beginning to tackle my situation with a new sense of resolve and acceptance. I was actually able to again think creatively and began to have a renewed zeal to get back into business. Dad and all of my family encouraged me. Things were beginning to get back to normal, or should I say, my new normal. With God once again by my side, though it was not *He* who had ever left but rather *me* placing my focus on other things, I realized for the first time in my life that it is not perfection that should be my ultimate goal, but progress, a life-changing tenet that I have used throughout my career. No matter if I am rich or poor, God loves me just the same, and with His help I can meet life's challenges head-on. Thanks to Ballard's words, my emotional state of mind and life indeed turned around, and he was one of the first people I called to thank once my emotional ordeal was over.

As my world got back into equilibrium, things were beginning to look up for me. I knew over time I would find another job, and I was actually content knowing that the meaning of life was not what you do but who you are, and how truly insignificant we are in relation to the greatness of God. One after another, good things were beginning to happen for me, not the least of which was an unexpected phone call from another former acquaintance and neighbor of mine, Richard Herrington, that proved to be such a blessing. He wanted to meet with me about a novel business idea he had to start a community bank right here in Middle Tennessee. He wanted me to become one of the early investors in the new business venture. After our three-hour lunch, I was in, though I didn't tell Richard that at the time.

I had lost almost every financial asset I had, and while I was able to clearly see the business opportunity, I still had to be very careful not to mortgage my family's future without a lot of additional thought and prayer. I invested much time discussing the idea of starting a new federally chartered bank with several different people that I had much confidence in, such as Uncle Jim, Dick, and, of course, my family. I did a good amount of market research to see if a new bank in Middle Tennessee, and especially in Franklin, Tennessee, which is a beautiful and historic small town located just twenty or so miles south of Nashville in Williamson County, would work for a new bank location. Within a few weeks, I went back to Richard and suggested to him that I was very interested, but only if I was an active partner in the new venture, not just a passive investor.

I was emotionally and physically ready for this new challenge. I said good-bye to depression, thanks to Mike Ballard, and hello to a new business opportunity, thanks to my faith; I will forever be grateful for both!

CHAPTER 7

My Wild Ride: Franklin National Bank

Tell me and I forget. Teach me and I remember. Involve me and I learn.—Benjamin Franklin

One might assume that my admiration and respect for Benjamin Franklin was the impetus behind the name of our new start-up community bank—Franklin National Bank. I sure wish that had been the case! But the truth is that we chose the name of the bank because of its prime location—Franklin, Tennessee. Franklin is known for its quaint small-town feel, vibrant town square, wonderful antique stores and restaurants, and bright, interesting, and friendly residents, not to mention a few well-known music and movie stars who called it home. It had also been the home to some excellent community banks in the past and had a very strong reputation for real quality community banking, but over the years that landscape changed dramatically.

A few years before we opened our bank, Franklin had been lucky to have three of the best community banks, including Williamson County Bank, Bank of Franklin, and Harpeth National Bank. Those were the days where people knew each other's names and everyone from the bank teller to the branch manager was accessible to customers almost twenty-four/seven. Believe it or not, Williamson County had developed a reputation around the state as having arguably the best community banks in all of Tennessee, if not the entire South. But like everything else in life, there is always a beginning and an end. And as the big banks began to gobble up the small community banks in the late 1990s, Franklin found itself in a place where it had virtually no community banks after enjoying so many years of business growth and prosperity.

But there were many exciting opportunities created by this new reality, and so I felt the time was right to seriously consider what was to become one of the best business decisions of my life.

One of the real benefits of having to live through a few months of clinical depression, as odd as that might sound, and coming out of it was that I learned the true meaning of life. While that might sound like a cliché, for anyone who has ever experienced the emotional ravages of depression, finding your place in the world can be quite daunting. So for me, life's meaning became simple and quite clear.

What that meant was having faith in God and knowing that I didn't have to be perfect, just do the best I could each and every day. Just like Pope Francis said in his address to a joint meeting of the US Congress on September 24, 2015, "Live by the Golden Rule." I have heard those words throughout my life, and I was ready to put to them to the test once again as I made the decision to get back into the game.

Yogi Berra, the great Yankees catcher in the early sixties, once said, "If you come to a fork in the road, take it." (By the way, I became a real fan of the New York Yankees about the age of nine when I learned that Mickey Mantle's birth date was October 20, the same day as mine.) I enjoyed playing baseball in both high school and college, and I always wore number seven since that was Mickey's uniform number. Yogi Berra's words couldn't have better applied to my own situation; now I was more than ready to take that fork in the road.

After that initial lunch meeting with my friend, Richard Herrington, one of my chief tasks was to secure investors for Franklin National Bank. I was confident that I would have some success finding them and convincing them that their initial investment would pay off in the not too distant future. We had a lot going for us in that sales pitch, too. First, all of the community banks in Franklin were bought up by the giant regional banks, and the folks in Franklin told us they were clearly not happy with their bureaucracy and the growing lack of personal connection as those banks continued to move more and more of the decision making to their headquarters in larger cities. Also, General Motors decided to open a new automotive plant in Williamson County which became a Saturn production facility, and so having the largest plant of its kind in the United States right in our own backyard was a real plus. With hundreds of new jobs on the horizon, folks who were going to work there would need places to live, and the company's suppliers would also open up shop nearby, adding to what we knew would be explosive growth in the area.

My meeting with our first potential investor, Eddy Richey, who was a longtime personal friend of mine, went very well. Eddy was a very successful entrepreneur in his own right and for many years had some great successes with businesses in insurance and the weight-loss industries. He was actually a co-owner in a business venture with Gordon Inman, owning and operating approximately sixty or so Nutri-System Weight Loss franchises. Additionally, Gordon was a very talented entrepreneur who owned several excellent properties in the area as well as owning the most successful real estate company in Franklin at the time. Most notably, Gordon actually owned a building right in the heart of the Franklin town square, a building that we believed would be a perfect location for our new bank and which ultimately became our headquarters and home office for Franklin National Bank.

As one of the initial investors, I had to put up $150,000 of my own money, which since coming out of near bankruptcy, and having some down time because of the depression, was a real challenge. But since I never lost my tenacity and drive, I was able to borrow the money from a variety of sources; I finally had skin in the game!

After our first meeting with Eddy, who quickly recognized the opportunity and who helped set up a meeting with Gordon, we were off and running even a little more quickly than I had initially anticipated. Both Eddy and Gordon soon made substantial financial commitments and ended up being the two largest shareholders in the bank. Other local Franklin and Middle Tennessee business executives, such as Wilson Overton, Steve Hall, Harold Pierce, and Ed Silva, all of whom were successful in other businesses, helped form our group of founders and the first board of directors. They shared our vision of wanting to recapture the magic of the down-home friendly spirit of the banks they had banked with in the past and sorely missed.

One by one, we were able to secure the funding we needed to get the new venture off of the ground. We had eight solid founding investors and were able to raise more than $6 million, all of which we knew we needed to build this business literally from the ground floor up. We had originally hoped to raise approximately $10 million, as we fully expected the bank stock to be something that would be a very hot commodity, even anticipating potentially an overdemand for the stock. Our premise was that the Franklin and Williamson County community had hoped to have great community banking back. However, the time frame that we were working to market the stock was shortly after the infamous Black Monday! (In the world of banking and finance, Black Monday refers to Monday, October 19, 1987, when virtually all of the stock markets around the world crashed, shedding incredible value in a very short time.)

The crash began in Hong Kong and spread west to Europe, quickly hitting the United States after other markets had already declined by a significant margin. The Dow Jones Industrial Average (DJIA) fell exactly 508 points to 1,738.74 (22.61 percent). In Australia and New Zealand, the 1987 crash is also referred to as "Black Tuesday," because of the time zone difference. The terms *Black Monday* and *Black Tuesday* are also applied to October 28 and October 29, 1929, respectively, which occurred after Black Thursday on October 24, which started the Stock Market Crash of 1929. So clearly there were issues with our timing in terms of convincing folks to make investments in our bank stock.

At the outset, we agreed that our ultimate goal would be to sell the bank to a larger regional or national bank at some point over the coming ten to fifteen years. While we would hopefully be making money for our initial founders and stockholders, we would also be preserving that personal touch and small-town feel that customers said they enjoyed about all of the community banks that were gobbled up by the big boys in prior years.

Even though I had been involved in a start-up business before, working to start and build SEC Reality Corporation with Dick Freeman, still this was the first time I actually had a major financial stake personally in a start-up business. It was also a very different experience for other reasons, too. I had to deal with seven spirited and distinct personalities, many of whom differed on issues such as what primary types of lending we should initially focus on, where we might eventually want to build branches, and whether we should seek to be a state-chartered bank or a federally chartered bank, to name a few.

And, since I was the youngest member of the investment group, I didn't quite have the track record of some of the major players, such as Gordon Inman, who eventually became the largest shareholder and was also chairman of the board. Gordon was at least fifteen years older than me and personally invested $3 million in our initial stock offering, thus becoming our largest shareholder. But I learned so much from Gordon, who was an especially savvy businessman. Though Gordon never graduated from college, he was and is exceptionally smart in business, having built several different and very successful companies over the years. He has always seemed to me to just have a sixth sense and be able to recognize trends and good business opportunities. Gordon ended up being one of the primary reasons why our bank turned out to be so profitable and successful. Frankly, I do not believe we would have ever experienced the ultimate success we were so blessed to achieve without his passion and involvement.

We also agreed during those initial meetings to establish the bank's management team and board of directors, and how we wanted to brand and market Franklin National Bank. We worked out the lease terms with Gordon for our headquarters facilities on the town square of Franklin, as he owned a great historic building that was strategically well positioned and just perfect for a start-up bank. We determined some key bankers at other banks we wanted to recruit for management positions. At times the discussions became somewhat intense, if not very heated, and I soon realized that dealing with a group of equal partners, many of whom were also my longtime friends, could be a real challenge.

One of our strengths as a team was that some of our founders and initial management personnel were individually strong in areas that the other team members were not. For example, we had former bankers, an attorney, a commercial real estate developer, a CPA, and other expertise in our group of founders. My strength was in sales and management, and having been in the commercial banking business, where I started my career, as well as having founded SEC Realty Corporation, I was fiscally conservative. Having been mentored by Dick Freeman and actually starting, building, and operating a highly successful business in the prior years, I understood well how to recruit, interview, and employ solid personnel and manage the cost side of running a profitable business.

I knew from experience that to run a successful business, you have to have a handle on the true cost of things. If not, you can run out of capital quickly, which would surely doom any business, especially a new one. I also had learned that many businesses fail because the owner/operator doesn't always have a strong enough knowledge of the total costs of running his or her business. Too many new business ventures are started by individuals who may have enjoyed great sales success with their prior employers but have never had to actually manage and operate a business on their own. They simply don't know what they don't know! While no one will ever operate a successful business without great sales, likewise savvy managers simply have to know their costs. If they are successful at bringing in a lot of business but are spending more money than they bring in, well, they are sure to ultimately fail. Successfully managing all the various expenses that any business has to encounter is absolutely critical to long-term business viability. It was an important business lesson, for sure.

I will never forget December 1, 1989, when we first opened the doors to Franklin National Bank. It was electric. People were waiting in long lines just to get in, and we prepped our team of approximately twenty employees to expect a large and steady stream of new customers throughout that day. They were up to the task, too. From Gordon Inman to Richard Herrington and all of us founders, we all were eager to greet our new customers with a smile, a brochure or two, and a chance to be a part of our opening day fanfare. I couldn't help but think about a childhood memory during that day, remembering the smell and enticing aroma of hot Krispy Kreme doughnuts as Dad drove Steve and me up and down the community streets of Woodbine knocking on neighbors' doors on those early Saturday mornings to sell doughnuts to raise money for our church. Maybe I should have brought a box or two over to the bank that day?

As I learned from Dick Freeman, timing, timing, timing means everything, and that certainly proved to be the case as we began our adventure as owners of the best community bank in all of Tennessee— Franklin National Bank. At least that is what we hoped at the outset. We opened the bank at just the right time, hired many of the best and brightest people, and had a location that was second to none. In addition, the economic conditions were improving and people were investing once again in home improvements and taking out loans for cars, college tuition, and a variety of other things, too. Over the next few years, as the Saturn plant became a reality, thousands of new jobs were created, and home sales in and around Franklin lit up! There could not have been a much better time to start a new bank.

The Tax Reform Act of 1986 was mostly felt by the commercial real estate owners and investors, and, of course, the savings and loans all across the country. Typical bank customer didn't feel the effects of the legislation nearly as much. They mostly felt the pain of that law via higher taxes, which were necessary to cover the costs of all the bank failures, though, as usual, these folks were told that it was the greedy bankers and the "big money folks" who caused all the initial pain.

But I was feeling a little bit of pain myself. And it had everything to do with a fellow named Chuck Lanier.

Chuck was a good-looking guy who was around my age at the time, I would say in his early thirties. He was about six feet tall and was a very impressive fellow with a great financial background. So in my role as executive vice president of the bank, I hired Chuck to become our senior lending officer. He was good at it, too. Soon he became the person responsible for approving or disapproving all of our major loan applications, and he had a lot of sway with the bank's senior executives. Basically, I kept hearing, "What Chuck says goes," and soon that created some tension between us. When I would bring a loan before our committee, Chuck would ask me a thousand questions, and at the time I felt he was singling me out in his interrogation. He would ask things such as, "Are you sure Mr. Jones gave us all the correct information," or "Mike, did you check Mr. Smith's employment history to see if he qualifies for such a large sum of money, and fully review the credit report?"

The man was starting to really get to me. Back then, I have to admit I was a bit too full of myself and thought Chuck was just asking me questions that were overly tough and directed at me personally because he was jealous.

We were butting heads almost every week; I didn't like it one bit! One day I asked him if we could discuss the Johnson file, and he gruffly looked me right in the eye and said that he was too busy. I thought to myself, *I'm an executive vice president, and I hired this guy, and he is treating me like this?*" So I asked him if I could have a word with him. "Chuck, it's obvious to me that you always seem to have problems with my loans. I think it is a personal thing, and I really don't like it. Maybe this bank is not big enough for both of us? And by the way, I'm not going anywhere!" That conversation made me feel better. Both of us continued to work together in relative harmony, though the underlying tension still persisted.

Despite some issues that I personally had with Chuck Lanier, our little community bank was still firing on all cylinders; there was no sign of slowing down. In fact, the growth of our bank was really taking off.

In the late 1990s, we began to see our initial investment really pay off. We were in business now for about ten years, and were humming along like Pop Carson's trusted lawnmower. A few other regional banks approached us wanting to buy the bank outright, but we never received the type of offer we wanted. There were a few of our board meetings where the discussions about selling certainly became a little interesting, to say the least! A couple of the offers in particular were very good. A few of the board members certainly wanted to take advantage, while others wanted to hold out. I wondered myself if we were holding out a little too long and might later regret not having taken one of these exceptional offers. Gordon just continued to believe there would be better opportunities ahead, and he was very persuasive in urging the board to be patient.

Over the years, I learned a lot about compromise and working with different types of personalities and opinions. As I've always said, being able to listen and respect others' opinions and concerns goes a long way to achieve a goal, especially one that could impact many people's financial future and stability. After losing almost everything myself in the late 1980s, that was something that I would never allow to happen again! I recall another one of my favorite Benjamin Franklin quotes: "We were all born ignorant, but one must work hard to remain stupid."

It was a cool day in 2003 in Franklin, Tennessee, when the board of directors met to discuss a very serious offer to buy our bank from Fifth Third Bank, headquartered in Cincinnati, Ohio. They were a very large regional bank with total assets in excess of $80 billion and with similar values to ours. (By the way, today they are valued at nearly $139 billion!) They wanted to keep our management team intact and stay local, and they had a senior management team in Ohio we had grown to respect.

It was several months from the time that the folks at Fifth Third Bank first approached us about selling, and today it was D-Day. While

I remained as the third-largest shareholder in the bank, I had resigned from the board just a few short years before because of a federal banking statue that required a director of a bank to not operate a business in direct competition with that same bank. By that time, I was operating a new venture, my mortgage company known as Churchill Mortgage Corporation (CMC), which I founded in 1992. Once Franklin National Bank decided to expand and open a branch in Brentwood, Tennessee, where CMC was headquartered, I was forced to either sell CMC or resign from the bank board. While I loved the bank and was highly involved as both a large shareholder and a director, that decision became rather easy, as CMC was growing dramatically, and I loved the challenge of this new venture. I resigned from the bank but continued to hold all of my stock, so as a result I was quite invested in its future.

And, of course, my departure clearly ended the feud that I had with the likes of Chuck Lanier!

The Board of Directors of Franklin National Bank assembled in the board room to officially vote on the sale of Franklin National Bank to Fifth Third Bank that afternoon. I so wished I could have been there, as the bank was quite a significant emotional part of me, as well as a huge part of my financial future. It was something that I had enjoyed helping build as well, and I also knew that a sale of this magnitude would make our investors very wealthy men.

The mood in the boardroom was a strange combination of elation and cautious optimism, according to some of my fellow board members. But at the appointed time that day, with the stroke of a black ballpoint pen, the deal was done. Of course, it took several months to gain the various federal regulators' approval and actually close the deal, but the price paid by Fifth Third Bank ended up being the highest multiple of any community bank in the nation, as far as we knew at the time. I understand that may in fact still be the record.

I had to catch my breath for a moment realizing that not only did we build a profitable and sustainable business, but from those initial investments, each of us as founders as well as our hundreds of shareholders walked away having made more money than we could probably have ever dreamed. Many individuals, including myself, made millions, something I could never have dreamed of doing in my early years in business.

It was the thrill of a lifetime for me, and somehow a subconscious affirmation of my self-worth. Well, yes and no. By the time we sold the bank, I had my faith in God back in spades, and also knew that money wasn't the sole source of my happiness. God had so richly blessed me in so many ways, and I was thrilled to have it back, don't get me wrong, but being a good steward meant that I needed to do more with it that I had in the past.

Over the years as I matured and grew, I often thought about Chuck Lanier and how badly I treated him. I occasionally ran into him in downtown Nashville or at the Cool Springs Galleria Mall, and we exchanged pleasantries, but that is about as far as it went. Then, tragically, for me and our entire family, in 2006 my mom passed away from kidney disease, a battle she heroically fought for years. I've heard the saying that you can judge the worth of a person by how many people attend their funeral. That must be true, because more than five thousand people came to Christ Church for her service. I was told later that nearly ten thousand people attended her wake. Mom was truly a one-of-a kind person, and there is not a day that goes by that I don't miss her and wish I could hear her voice again asking me, "Mike, how was your day, and what the kids are up to?"

There is a sweet story about Mom that illustrates her quintessential humor and compassion. When she realized that her kidney disease was progressing, and there was no real sign of hope, she did something most people would never dream of doing. She put together a list. No, it wasn't a list of her most valuable possessions or a list of who would get her most treasured items. No. It was a list of potential *wives* for Dad. Women in our church who Mom thought would be best for Dad when she was no longer around. She was so determined to make this venture a success that she asked me to come over to their house one day to go over it with her in detail. "Mike, your Dad and I have been together over fifty years, and I'm very afraid that he won't be able to manage without a woman in his life after I'm gone," she told me, as I listened to her with a feeling of sadness but also intense curiosity. "Dad won't do well alone," she said, and, "Mike, I'm okay with that. So here's a list of the women I would be good with in order of my preference." I was dumbfounded, but knowing Mom the way I did, I quickly realized that her plan was a thoughtful and selfless gesture that most women would probably never even consider.

So Mom reached into her pocket and gave me her handwritten list of five women's names. The number one on that list was Carol Bryant. Mom knew and loved Carol and believed that she and Dad would make a terrific couple. Carol was a former fashion model, was active in the church, and was someone Mom admired as well. As I read the list, I couldn't help smiling, and though Mom only lived another year after writing it, at that moment I was deeply touched by her selfless love and concern for her husband and best friend.

As the years went on, Carol did in fact become part of our family, and I am blessed that she is in our lives; we are all thankful for her each and every day. I'm convinced that Dad is still in good health and active and engaged as ever because of her devotion and love. Carol also has a great sense of humor, and I'm sure that was put to the test during a special tribute to Mom that we held at the church on January, 1, 2012.

It took place on Sunday afternoon. Dad was retired as pastor of Christ Church, and the senior pastor, Dan Scott, officiated the ceremony and the special tribute to Mom. We brought in the actual kitchen table that Dad reconfigured for their home, back when they were first married. Mom was good at repurposing things, and their kitchen table was formally a cedar wood picnic table that she found somewhere and thought would be perfect for their home. She lovingly antiqued it, giving it a weathered look, and we spent many days and nights sitting around that table together as a family. They are memories that I cherish to this day.

The kitchen table was carefully placed on the platform in the center of the pulpit, which served as the centerpiece of the event. Around the table were me, Steve, Dad, Pastor Scott, and Witsie. I sat on the left end, Pastor Scott was on the right end, and Witsie and Dad sat on each side. Pastor Scott interviewed each of us, asking us questions such as, "Reverend, how old where you when you founded Christ Church, and how did you manage to do that at eighteen years old?" Or he would ask Witsie, "You were just like a sister to the Hardwick boys. What was it like growing up with them?" We shared so many of our heartfelt memories of Mom, and throughout the two-hour event we laughed and cried like babies.

There must have been over twenty-five hundred people there, including Carol, who by this time was Dad's wife. So I decided to end the tribute by telling the story of Mom's list, knowing Carol would be the first one to know what I was about to say. I got up from the table and stood on the edge of the platform and said, "Thank you all for coming here today to honor Mom. As some of you may remember, Mom was a very organized and disciplined person. She kept lists of everything, including the women she wanted Dad to marry in the event of her death." I could see the puzzled looks on their faces as I reached into my pocket and pulled out that little piece of paper that had the women's names in order of Mom's preference. "Here is the list that Mom gave me about a year before she passed, and on it are the names of the women she wanted Dad to marry when she was no longer around. Guess whose name was number one? It was Carol Bryant." The crowd roared with laughter, including Carol, who was sitting in the front row. "As most of you know, that worked out pretty well for Dad! But I'm sure many of you are curious as to whom the other four women were who Mom handpicked for Dad." As I held the paper up to my eyes, ready to read the names of the unlucky four who never made the cut, I lowered it slowly and put it back into my pocket. The looks on their faces were priceless. "Well, folks, that will be a secret forever!"

Mom was so beloved, and that was evident from the thousands of people who attended her funeral service and the thousands more who came to her tribute event. It was a testament to her universal appeal.

Chuck Lanier was one of those people who came to Mom's funeral service. I had no idea he was there!

In fact, how I found out about it was about three weeks after the service, I got a beautiful sympathy card from Chuck that read, "I am so sorry for your loss, Mike. I never met your mother, but wish I had. I heard she was a wonderful lady, and I want to express my deepest sympathy to you and your family."

Oh, Lord, you really convicted me. I was so wrong to treat Chuck that way. He was just trying to do his job and probably saved the bank a lot of money because he did his job that well, I thought to myself after reading his heartfelt message. I knew I was wrong, but I did learn a great lesson that day, and that was to be kind to everyone and treat them with dignity—even if that meant checking my oversized ego at the door!

I finally decided to bury the hatchet and give Chuck a call. "Chuck, hi, this is Mike, and I want to thank you for coming to Mom's service. That was big of you," I said, getting up the courage to apologize for my bad and selfish behavior.

"Mike, thank you, but you don't have to apologize at all; you don't owe me anything," he said.

"Chuck, I also want to tell you that I owe you a big apology. Several years ago I treated you poorly while we were working together at Franklin National Bank, and I'm sorry for that," I told him. I felt that I needed to explain my behavior further, so I said, "Chuck I have to tell you why I did what I did. I was wrong, and you are a far better man than me. I want to make things right, Chuck, and I hope you will forgive me."

Chuck taught me a life lesson that day that I would never forget. He made me realize that despite any business success you may think you have, true success is not so much about how much money you make, how powerful you are, or what fancy car you drive. It is about treating people right, learning, growing, and taking time for self-reflection. It really is just trying to live by the Golden Rule. It's as simple as that. Like Benjamin Franklin said, "An investment in knowledge pays the best interest." I was determined to put that to the test, and, sure enough, I would have an opportunity to do just that as Churchill Mortgage got it wings and started to take off.

I will always be grateful for Chuck Lanier and what he taught me about the generosity of the soul and the power of forgiveness.

Chapter 8

Building a Corporate Culture that Puts People over Profits

Among the things you can give and still keep are your word, a smile, and a grateful heart.—Zig Ziglar

If there is one thing I have learned from working in corporate America, starting a bank from the ground up with my seven business partners and getting to know people from all walks of life, it is this: follow the Golden Rule, celebrate a good idea, keep a long view of life and not be a day trader, and show respect and honor for others. It's really that simple.

Over the years, people have always asked me how I was able to build a corporate culture based on those values, and, at the same time, build a profitable and sustainable business. I have always considered myself to be what some would refer to as lucky, but what I would much rather say, a blessed man. While my brother, Steve, and I grew up with a relatively modest lifestyle, our family was rich in love and compassion. Dad and Mom were givers in the truest sense of the word. Watching them day to day care for us, thousands of Christ Church families, and the Nashville community at large, while at the same time maintaining a deeply loving marriage relationship with each other, gave my brother and me a deep sense of responsibility to make the lives of others better.

I also share with Dad a voracious love of learning. Growing up, I would watch him sitting in the family den night after night reading books as I was getting ready for bed. Once he finished spending roughly twenty hours preparing his weekly sermon, he would devour books on a wide range of subjects—not necessarily always congruent—such as philosophy, business, politics, history, music, and religion, to name a few. To this day, he hasn't lost his passion for knowledge, and though he has slowed down a bit because of his age, the sparkle in his eyes is just as bright when he recounts the highlights and memories of a life well-lived.

I am also blessed to have inherited Dad's curiosity and tenacity. As an adult, I realized what Dad was able to accomplish—not with quick fixes or gimmicks but rather with hard work, putting one step in front of the other each and every day to build one of the most successful megachurches in Middle Tennessee and, I dare say, anywhere in the United States, at least during that era. In fact, Dad defied the longevity of most pastors in his field. In a June 2014 study conducted by Dr. Franklin Dumond, the average tenure of a pastor in a local church is 3.6 years, and some other studies have suggested their tenure is a little bit longer, between five and seven years. That's why it is so remarkable that Dad served as the founder and senior pastor of Christ Church Nashville for more than sixty years!

So when I was thinking about starting my next totally independent business venture—a mortgage brokerage—I wanted to do it on my terms but employ some of the most successful lessons I learned from Dad, as well as what I saw firsthand that clearly didn't work. I hoped to create an environment where I could bring all of the core values I had learned and lived by all of my life to a business setting of my own. I did realize, however, that would be a challenge although I had read many books on corporate cultures and their successes and failures, and so had a definite idea of what I wanted to accomplish with my new venture.

But first I had to come up with a name. Rather than simply calling my company Hardwick Mortgage, I decided that it had to be someone or something greater than myself. It had to reflect my core values of honor and respect and, at the same time, have a strong and powerful presence of stability. One day it hit me like a ton of bricks. I'm going to call my company Churchill Mortgage. It combined my unwavering admiration for one of the greatest leaders of the twentieth century—Winston Churchill—and also embodied my love and devotion to our church.

I admire Winston Churchill for a thousand reasons. Chief among them was his brilliance, tenacity, political courage, and amazing communications skills. In the 1930s, he was the first person who warned about the rise of Adolf Hitler and Nazi Germany, and during the Second World War, in his role as first lord of the admiralty, he refused to surrender and helped inspire British resistance and opposition to the Nazi regime. This Nobel Prize winner, patriot, political icon, and wartime hero was just the inspirational figure I would be proud to have as a moniker for my start-up new venture. Churchill once said: "Courage is what it takes to sit down and listen."

With those words in mind, I sat down with my notebook early one morning, as I do almost each and every weekday, and jotted down some thoughts about what I wanted Churchill Mortgage to be—for my employees and potential customers. I would often randomly discuss my thoughts with folks I had great confidence in because of their past successes. I had my business plan down pat—no worries on that front. However, building a culture that puts people over profits and creating an atmosphere of teamwork and trust sounds good on paper but in actuality is a challenge to implement. Having said that, I was inspired and motivated again by Churchill's words, "We may make a living by what we get, but we make a life by what we give."

I kept scribbling down notes from my thoughts for about a week and came up with some of the top choices for the core values that I wanted all of the Churchill family to share. They were always percolating in my mind, even though in the early days of my company they needed to take a backseat until I had all of the business issues resolved, such as incorporation, infrastructure, employees, marketing materials, etc. I knew deep in my heart that sooner rather than later I would build a corporate culture on my own terms. Though it wouldn't be easy, I was comforted by a quote from Frances Hesselbein that my good friend and sales management guru, Tom Black, shared with me about culture change. Hesselbein said, "Culture does not change because we desire to change it. Culture changes when the organization is transformed: the culture reflects the realities of people working together every day."

I will never forget that cool clear early spring morning on March 13, 1992, when I first put my key into the second floor of my new office space located at 761 Old Hickory Boulevard in Brentwood, Tennessee, about fifteen minutes or so from downtown Nashville. I was just forty years old and ready for this new chapter in my life. While we only occupied one thousand square feet of the building, and there were only two of us, I still felt the excitement just like I used to at Christmastime, not being able to sleep in anticipation of what the morning would bring. My gifts this time were more directed outward than inward. If I could use all my skills and experience to create a business that truly put people over profits, while also being able to build an extremely profitable enterprise, then in my mind I would have accomplished my goal.

For me, that meant that my future employees should ultimately have a good heart and care about other people. It was the way I was reared, and I saw how that translated into success in work and life for Dad and Mom, as well as for my grandparents and so many other family members I most admired.

As I often do, I thought about scripture and the story about Abraham in Genesis 20:2, in particular. Abraham was a fellow who was willing to lie about his own wife, Sarah, telling others that she was not his wife but, rather, his sister. In fact, he did this on not one, but two occasions. Abraham did this because of his fear of being killed himself, but he soon realized the error of his ways, and he did the right thing by finally setting the record straight. He was not a man of perfection. Far from it, but he was someone who just kept on trying until he did the right thing. Abraham kept chopping wood!

Neither of my grandfathers were men of great wealth, either. But they were rich in many other ways because they always tried to do the right thing, just like Abraham. By raising their own children to be caring, loving, and generous people, God blessed them in ways that were much more important than just money. Their children grew up to be wonderful people, influencing tens of thousands of others and passing along their own individual values of kindness, patience, empathy, goodness, caring for others, and giving both their time and resources to the people they met along the way in their lives. It was another position in my playbook of life that gave me the confidence to know that this experiment of mine could work.

While at the time I didn't necessarily have a crystal ball to see what Churchill Mortgage would eventually grow into, I did know that I wanted to build a successful business, one that would make money and help provide solid employment income for everyone, but also give richness to our employees' lives because of a culture that rewards both their business success with their personal commitment to others.

It was within the first eight to ten months that we grew very quickly, from our initial two employees to a small business with nine employees. Stephanie Christian, who joined Churchill Mortgage right out of college during our first year in business, and who is now one of our more successful loan officers and a great friend, reminded me recently that I said to her in those early days of the business, "Stephanie, I can teach a person the mortgage business and how to process loans, but I can't take a dishonest person and make him or her honest. I cannot take someone who is basically contentious and make him or her harmonious. I hope all of our employees that we hire will have character and integrity." She certainly has quite an impressive long-term memory, too, as that conversation took place over two decades ago.

I talked often to our employees about the high value of always telling the truth, being honest and forthright with our customers, and just basically doing the right thing, even when it may cost us money. I felt then, as I do now, that always trying to live out those core beliefs ultimately provides a sense of calm, peace, and contentment and oftentimes provides benefits beyond that, such as a good income and personal satisfaction. Communication was also essential to translating our value system to new hires and reinforcing them day in and day out with our existing employee base. It has been said that 90 percent of all problems are usually a result of either a lack of communication or a miscommunication.

Years later, once we had grown considerably and things were humming along and I had most of my management team in place, I literally spent a full week holed up in a large conference room off-site with a few of our senior managers, including Matt Clarke, Doug Walker, Josh Phillips, and a couple of other folks, really listening and thinking deeply about our core values with the intention of actually articulating them to our employees in writing. The team came up with these core foundations following that meeting. They included trustworthiness, empathy, life balance, integrity, excellence, dedication, stewardship, humility, lifelong learning, the heart of a teacher, philanthropy, and, of course, the "broomsweeper." I recalled the lessons I learned from all of my mentors and tried to combine those with some of the business leaders I admired, such as Dick Freeman, Dave Ramsey, John Maxwell, Joe Stumpf, Todd Duncan, Zig Ziglar, Cecil Kemp, and so many others. My ultimate goal was not to be a pioneer, but rather someone who has learned from those who have come before me so I could avoid those inevitable arrows that were sure to come my way when undertaking such a different way of doing business than I had experienced in the past.

I was determined and, need I say, driven, to make Churchill Mortgage a place where employees could thrive as individuals and also become part of a family business that would not only create wealth for people in top management, but shared prosperity for everyone, from the receptionist to the chief financial officer. In addition, I was passionate about bringing faith into the business, not necessarily driven by any particular religious affiliation, but rather the basic principles of the Golden Rule. It would be a delicate balance for sure, but as Churchill said so eloquently: "A pessimist sees the difficulty in every opportunity; an optimist sees the opportunity in every difficulty."

By 1996, we were growing rapidly, and Churchill Mortgage went from a start-up business with only a handful of employees and one physical office, to being licensed to transact business in approximately eight states and an employee base of more than forty people. It was very important for me to get the hiring process right, in addition to communicating our core values to each and every new employee. We also needed a humane process of letting those employees who were not performing well exit, or if they were just simply not a good fit. It was also very important for me to be personally involved in the hiring and firing process and not delegate that responsibility to a human relations manager, especially during Churchill's formative years.

But how would I be able to tell if a prospective employee would fit in our value-based culture? How could I surmise if someone was just giving me lip service, or if he or she was sincere and had the personality traits that I knew were needed to perform well in our type of business culture? Once again I turned to my heroes, and scripture, to help me devise a plan.

I thought to myself, *Dad and Mom always had hoped I would follow in their footsteps and become a pastor. Well isn't it interesting that in a sense I am a pastor, and my church is called Churchill Mortgage! My congregation is my employees, and I want everyone to excel not just at work but in life, too.* Part of being a good pastor and certainly a good leader, as Winston Churchill said, is having the ability to listen. Dad certainly had that skill well-developed as I had observed over the years. Part of that listening skill, I thought, was also being able to ask the right questions—to dig deeper into a person's life in order to uncover who he or she really is at the core. If a person's heart is full of love and compassion, and if he or she truly cares about others and not just himself or herself, then the person would at least make it through the first round of interviews. I also knew that if this culture was going to work, I had to lead by example.

I came up with a list of questions that I would ask potential employees, and as I've heard many times over the past twenty years from people who have worked for me, "Mike, no one has ever asked me about who I am as a person during a job interview." Here's one of the early conversations I had with Joshua Phillips when he first came to me for a job in 1998. "Joshua, hey, thanks for coming in today. While you are a young man, you still have an impressive background, and it looks like you have some limited mortgage sales experience," I said.

"Thank you, Mr. Hardwick," he replied, and I could see the nervousness on his face.

"So I hear you have four children. That must be a real challenge. How are you able to balance your responsibilities at home with those at work?"

"Well, Mr. Hardwick, I try to make it work because it is important to me. My wife and I try very hard to make sure our family comes first. While I work long hours and I'm happy to do that, my first responsibility is to support my family. I love working, and I know I could be a real asset to your team here at Churchill."

Needless to say, Joshua got the job! Not surprisingly, he became one of our top loan originators over the ensuing years. In fact, after successfully working for us for a number of years, he was recruited by a competitor, and, much to my dismay, he took the job. I was heartbroken at the time when he left, but I always believed that everyone should not be afraid to pursue their dreams, even if they are at our expense. For me to hold someone back just because of my own selfish wants and needs would be wrong. I have always tried to create in my employees a feeling that they can come and talk with me about other opportunities they are being offered, knowing that I will give them my best insight without any regard for my own selfish desires. My interest was in them first. While I truly hated to see Joshua leave at that time, it appeared that the opportunity for him and his family was probably best for them.

My father has taught me so many things over the years, and one particular lesson was to never burn bridges! I stayed in touch with Joshua and continued to connect with him about once every month or so just to mentor him and keep in touch. Just because he wasn't working for me didn't mean that we couldn't still be friends.

Unfortunately for Josh and many of his employees, in 2008 the company he was working for folded, and he suddenly found himself out of a job. He reached out to me and asked if we could absorb him and a few of his employees, but at that particular time I felt from an operational standpoint we could not successfully support that option. I didn't want to let him down or hurt his team, so instead of bringing him back to Churchill, I helped him relocate with another good company. Of course, I suggested to him that at some point in the future we *would* be in a position to provide him the type of strong operational support that any good mortgage production team needs, and I was hopeful that he would consider rejoining us at that point in the future. Needless to say, about fifteen or so months later, in January 2010, I offered him his old job back. We were all thrilled when Joshua decided to come back to work for us and was once again part of our Churchill family.

A couple of years after he returned, we also learned the heartbreaking news that his sixteen-year-old son, Jesse, was in desperate need of a heart transplant; our entire team came together to pray for him. I had known Jesse, as well as his brother and two sisters, since they were just little children. We all loved and cared so much for Joshua and his sweet wife, Amy, and their children, as they had become a significant part of our Churchill Mortgage family. As a result, we decided to help support him and his family financially during his time of need, as he would not be able to fully focus his time on his job. I said: "Joshua, we love you and your family, and I want you to know that we will help take care of you. Don't overly worry about your business right now; just focus on your son." This is what we call "servant leadership." But even more than that, it is leading by example and making sure that what you are asking from your employees, you are also asking of yourself. Josh continued to do a great job while spending the necessary time with his family taking care of Jesse, and things worked out well.

I was very pleased with how things were going. It took a few years, but I soon realized that our corporate culture was actually working, and my employees were beginning to take their commitment to the community and each other seriously. By creating our core foundations with input from our team, communicating those almost every day through our internal and external sources, as well as leading by example, my dream was coming true.

I'm sure some of my peers in the mortgage banking business would call me crazy for doing this, but I also had an unorthodox way of dealing with those mortgage customers who were simply not in a strong enough financial shape to successfully apply for a loan. Since one of our cultural core values is to have empathy for others and to have the heart of a teacher, we worked together on a way to help those in tough financial shape to get back on their feet. This is a typical response from one of our loan officers who has just told an applicant that they could not receive a mortgage from Churchill. "Hello, Mr. Smith, I am calling to tell you that we, unfortunately, cannot give you a mortgage at this time. But we have been reviewing your credit history and want to help you get back on your feet. I see you are presently carrying too much debt in relation to your monthly earnings. We have some excellent tools we can provide you to help you reverse that trend. In fact, we would be happy to talk with you regularly if you need our help, and we will also send you a comprehensive package that includes tools and helpful information to turn your financial situation around. We believe in you, Mr. Smith, and believe you can be successful in your efforts. We would like to be your accountability partner to help you in the future improve your present financial condition."

Not only does this approach make good business sense—after all, Mr. Smith may come back to us someday and be able to qualify for a loan as well as tell others about us—but on a personal level, we are giving back to others and helping them better their lives.

As we continued to grow—today now licensed in about forty states with nearly four hundred employees—it was crystal clear to me that I needed to find a chief operating officer who could help me manage this explosive growth and someone who was also a person with great integrity and heart. I was looking for a natural leader with stellar financial and management skills and also a person with faith, compassion, and a deep love for people. I found that person and more in Matt Clarke.

Matt had a successful career in insurance and finance, plus he was just genuinely a nice guy. When he came in for his first interview in the middle of 2003, I asked him the same sort of questions that I asked all of my employees over the years. "Matt, tell me a little bit about your family. Where do your parents and siblings live, and how often do you all have the opportunity to see each other? What brought you to Nashville from Boston?" I could see in his steel blue eyes that he was slightly taken aback, but he quickly rallied and told me all about his life, what he believed in and stood for, and his hopes and dreams for the future. He, surprisingly, even told me that he came to Nashville looking for two things, good barbecue and a pretty wife! Well, he ended up with both!

As he spoke lovingly and fondly about his wife, Valerie, and their two sons, Seth and Logan, his parents and siblings, how he loved spending time with them, and how appreciative he was of the opportunities his parents afforded him, I knew at that moment that he was the right guy for the job, and he would help perpetuate our culture and, even more than that, embrace it in his heart and soul. Of course, I liked his resume and checked out all of his references as any good businessperson would do, but most important to me was getting to know what type of person he really was.

I have taken many of John Maxwell's courses, including one on transformational leadership. Maxwell is a renowned international speaker and management expert who has also been an inspiration to me over my business career. He asserts that transformational leaders share a number of traits that make them successful. Some of those include: the ability to be transformed, connecting with those who have a common purpose, tapping into people's creativity, and putting all of those qualities and more into practice. Putting into practice those type qualities is often difficult, for sure, but as Winston Churchill said: "Success is not final, failure is not fatal: it is the courage to continue that counts."

Matt fit in just fine. Over the years, I have slowly entrusted more and more of our leadership responsibilities at Churchill to Matt. He has earned my confidence and trust, and he has been able to continue our legacy of integrating our special corporate culture into the everyday lives of our employees. He has also helped bring that unique caring spirit of Churchill Mortgage into the local communities where we operate. In fact, I am extremely proud and honored to say that Matt was recognized as the CFO of the Year in 2015 by the *Nashville Business Journal* for midsized businesses in Middle Tennessee!

"There are so many things I learned from Mike over the years," said Matt. "I've learned to be a better listener, provide leadership through service, be the same good person at work and at home, work harder than the next guy, be an expert and surround yourself with other experts, be committed to lifelong continual learning, serve others without exception, and do what you do with great joy. Mike has also shown me by example that no matter what happens during the course of any business day, always end that day with a smile. Most of all, Mike has been the most influential mentor in my life. He's invested in me, and also I try to pass those lessons I have learned from him along to our employees. As Mike is fond of saying, 'We don't expect people to be perfect, because we are not perfect.' We simply ask our teammates to keep their eyes on the doughnut not the hole. Keep focusing on the big picture and don't allow molehills to become mountains. Don't ask someone to do something that you wouldn't do yourself. He's also said many, many times, 'Things are rarely ever as good as they seem or as bad as they seem.' That is quintessential Mike Hardwick."

Clearly, Matt is in the game!

Under Matt's increasing influence and leadership, we've been able to effectively implement the Churchill culture to assure it continues long after I am gone. These are some of the things I did to make that happen.

First, I have found that the most effective method, and quite possibly the only one that works long term, is to spend a lot of time with the next management person in line. By that I mean I have taken Matt with me on business trips where we would sit for long hours on an airplane and just talk shop. Our families have enjoyed many vacation trips together to places such as Lake Tahoe for snow skiing, and Hawaii and the Caribbean for fun beach times and great golf, where we are able to really spend both quality and quantity time just growing our relationship. I have brought Matt with me on countless lunches where I have met with customers, bankers, and other employees so he can watch and listen. Afterward, I would usually ask him for his thoughts and try to engage him in the hows and whys of my decisions. We have also enjoyed taking part in Dave Ramsey's Entrepreneur Leadership Master Series, Todd Duncan's Annual Sales Mastery events in Palm Springs, California, and his Achieving Leadership Excellence weeklong training on many occasions over the past several years.

I have also been coaching managers for years on how to spend time with employees who have messed up, helping them learn from a failure or mistake and not beating them up emotionally. I am proud to say that we typically don't have many employees making the same mistake over and over again because of showing them mercy and using the experience as a teachable moment. I have also done that with most of my key managers over the years as well, until I felt that the decisions they made were quite similar to what I would have done in that particular situation. Incidentally, Matt and I have been doing the same thing with my son, Lawson. For the last few years we've been preparing him to help lead Churchill Mortgage in the future, and I know that Matt does it often with our other Churchill Mortgage senior managers, as well.

While it clearly takes more time and commitment from me, and, of course, now Matt, it has paid off in countless ways. Our team managers know who we are, what we stand for, how we make decisions, and how we differentiate between mountains and molehills. They also live and breathe our core foundation values and know they are part of something greater than themselves. Every person who works at Churchill knows that we care. I remember Theodore Roosevelt's great quote when he said: "Folks don't care how much you know until they know how much you care!"

They have also seen firsthand those guiding principles in action.

For example, one young loan officer came to her supervisor and was in tears. Why? She had closed a loan but miscalculated the numbers, and it was clear to her that we were going to have to take about a $3,500 loss. As the story was told to me by her supervisor, she was totally distraught and apologized profusely, even saying that we had every right to fire her for her lack of attention to detail. Instead of taking her to the proverbial woodshed, her supervisor said this: "You know, we all make mistakes sometimes. Let's walk through what happened and see where we can improve in the future. We want to learn from this so we don't repeat the same mistake. Churchill Mortgage will cover the loss, so don't worry, it's not the end of the world. You'll make it right next time."

Another time, a single woman applying for a mortgage loan was taken under the wing of one of our longtime employees named Sherri. This sweet lady was fifty-six years old and had never owned a home or an automobile, though she had been working at Vanderbilt Hospital at that time for approximately twenty-six years. Sherri invested considerable time working with her to get in a position to be able to buy her first home, and the woman was extremely grateful for the love and support. Though she didn't have a car and worked full-time, she was so appreciative that she took several buses to come to our office and thank Sherry in person just a few days after the closing of her loan.

It gives me such pride to know that we are teaching by example.

"I have watched Mike give his heart and soul to us," added Stephanie. "I was one of his first employees and am now his longest-tenured employee, and I can say without a doubt that he is the real deal. He would give you the shirt off of his back, and there isn't a soul in this world he wouldn't reach out and help. As an employee, I'm so proud to work in a company that has these kinds of values. One Christmas we were contemplating a gift for Mike, a man who has everything. He asked us not to do that anymore but instead reach out to someone in need, and that would make him the happiest. That started an annual tradition of giving out what we call 'blessing baskets,' mentoring at-risk youth, providing food for the hungry, and so much more."

When I hear those words from my wonderful work family, I am humbled. Recently some of them were interviewed and asked what words they felt described the values and culture of Churchill Mortgage. Here's what they said: "humility, love, trust, karma, humor, authentic, generous, family, integrity, caring, purposeful, attitude, grace, levity, faith, stewardship, balance, and profit with purpose."

Our Churchill Core Foundations by definition have their stated meaning. I want to share those Webster Dictionary definitions, and juxtapose how we've defined them for our employees and integrated them into our everyday business lives.

1. **Honesty.** (noun) The quality of being honest. To us it means: providing truthful information, even when it is unpopular.
2. **Humility.** (noun) A modest or low view of one's own importance. To us it means: putting the interest of others above personal gain.
3. **Integrity.** (noun) The quality of being honest and having strong moral principles. To us it means: doing the right thing, all the time.
4. **Teacher.** (noun) A person who teaches, especially in a school. To us, the "Heart of a Teacher" means: willing to take the time to help customers make sound decisions.
5. **Attitude.** (noun) A settled way of thinking or feeling about someone or something. To us it means: hopeful, positive, determined, team player, respectful, kind.
6. **Stewardship.** (noun) The office of duties and obligations of a steward. To us it means: responsible management of entrusted resources.
7. **Philanthropy.** (noun) The desire to promote the welfare of others, expressed by the generous donation of money to good causes. To us it means: giving of personal time and talents.

8. **Lifelong learning**. (noun) The provision or use of both formal and informal learning opportunities throughout people's lives. To us it means: continuous pursuit of expanding personal knowledge both on and off the job.

9. **Life balance**. (noun) A comfortable state of equilibrium achieved between an employees' primary priorities of their employment position and their private lifestyle. To us it means: while work is important, it is not everything.

10. **Broomsweeper**. (noun) It is our own definition. It means: helping others in need and being a team player…whoever is closest to the broom, sweeps!

The great Winston Churchill was once asked to describe his thoughts about freedom and hope, and here's what he said: "All the great things are simple, and many can be expressed in a single word: freedom, justice, honor, duty, mercy, hope."

As I look back at the type of caring and purposeful culture I have tried to build in Churchill's honor and that of my parents, uncles, and mentors here at Churchill Mortgage, I deeply hope and pray that I have made a difference. Mission statements, goals, and objectives all help to provide a business with direction, but they will only be empty words unless they are backed up by the actions of their leaders. True leadership, as Churchill said, is simple. For me, it has always been and will always be faith, love, hope, and joy. Those are some of the words I sincerely try to live by each and every day.

CHAPTER 9

Family Matters in the Workplace: The Churchill Promise

> The two most important days in your life are the day you are born and the day you find out why.—Mark Twain

It has been said many times over the years that nothing is more important than *family*. Pope Francis during his visit to the United States in September 2015 kept extolling the importance of the family in almost every inspirational address he made before thousands of adoring crowds in Washington, DC; New York City; and Philadelphia. He said, "Families are factories of hope, and in families there is always light."

Of course I was blessed to have learned the importance of the family unit and human beings in general from Dad and Mom. Dad told me, "Son, always try to put people over property." And in this great country of ours, we have many definitions of what the family unit really embodies from those with both parents intact to single-parent homes, as well as too often those where parents are absent because of death or other reasons. Thankfully, folks in these circumstances many times are able to find family in their church or work community. It is my belief that every human being on God's great earth has the potential to do monumental things and be part of something larger than himself or herself. That is the essence of teamwork. Steve Jobs once said in a quote I just love: "Technology is nothing. What's important is that you have faith in people, that they are basically good and smart, and if you give them tools, they'll do wonderful things with them."

One of the great challenges any business leader faces is how to bring a disparate group of people together, many of whom come with different values, worldviews, religions and creeds, and even styles of communication. How can such a diverse group of individuals come together and share common values in an effort to achieve a unified goal? And how can employees learn to be caring team members, and biological family members be integrated successfully into a business setting?

These were all questions I asked myself over and over again as Churchill Mortgage began to grow. Matt and I strategized many times about how we could keep our corporate culture relevant, pass along our core values down through the ranks, and at the same time, bring my children—Lawson, Megan, Shayna, and Michael—into the fold, if they chose to become involved in the business.

As anyone who owns a family business knows firsthand, it is one of the most daunting pursuits in terms of making sure it thrives from generation to generation. In fact, in a 2012 *Harvard Business Review* study, the data supports that premise. "Some seventy percent of family-owned businesses fail or are sold before the second generation has a chance to take over. Just ten percent remain active, privately held companies for the third generation to lead. In contrast to publicly held firms in which the average CEO tenure is six years, many family businesses have the same leaders for twenty or twenty-five years or longer, and these extended tenures can increase difficulties of coping with shifts in technology, business models, and consumer behavior."

I was not going to let Churchill Mortgage fall into that trap. On the contrary, I made a bold business decision in 2013 that would head that problem off at the pass and one that truly changed the lives of all of our employees—including my four children forever; but more about that later.

One of my favorite management and sales gurus and a wonderful personal friend—Tom Black—wrote about the idea that all people need and want to have *dreams*. He uses this quote by Pablo Picasso to illustrate that premise: "My mother said to me: 'If you become a soldier, you'll be a general, if you become a monk you'll end up as a pope.' Instead, I became a painter and wound up as Picasso." Pope Francis echoed Picasso's sentiment when he said, "I am happy that America continues to be for many a land of dreams; dreams which lead to action, to participation, to commitment; dreams which awaken what is deepest and truest in the life of people."

As most everyone who knows me realizes, I am a sports fanatic. I just love the competitive nature of football, basketball, and baseball, and the quiet resolve and tenacity of golf. I was privileged to be able to play baseball both in high school and college, as well as play and coach a great fast-pitch softball team for more than twenty years until my old body just wouldn't go anymore at the age of forty-three! Sports also figures deeply and truly in the life of the American people. Athletes, like anyone in any field who is successful, know how much hard work and determination play in taking a person over the top; someone just like Josh Robinson.

One might ask, "Who is Josh Robinson?" Josh Robinson, number 34, is a twenty-three-year-old running back for the Indianapolis Colts. He was drafted in the sixth round of the 2015 NFL Draft and was their 206th pick. At only five feet nine, he was an unlikely choice, but with a sturdy 225-pound frame, he was, nonetheless, fierce and competitive. No one knew, though, that this star athlete was homeless.

Like so many children and young adults across the country, Josh was a horrific statistic. NBC News recently reported that one in thirty American children was homeless at some point last year. That is about 2.5 million children, according to the National Center of Family Homelessness. And what's worse, the study also said that over half of those homeless children are younger than six years old.

Josh grew up with no parents at home at all. He never knew his father, and his mother was locked up in jail for most of his life for many serious offenses. He was bounced around from one foster home to another, and he estimates that he stayed in twenty different households over his young life. He even lived in the backseat of an old Nissan car given to him by his uncle while he was in high school in Franklinton, Louisiana. But what Josh lacked in living securely, he made up for with his giant heart, drive, and determination. Josh had dreams! Despite such personal trauma, Josh was a two-sport athlete in football and track, leading his team to the 4A state championship.

Luckily for Josh, his grandmother stepped up to the plate and took him in to live with her. She was a warm and generous woman who provided Josh with a loving and stable environment. Sadly, she passed away when he was just eleven years old.

But her love and compassion stayed with Josh as he grew up, and his spirit was never affected by his rocky and tumultuous home life.

Josh entered Mississippi State University on a Pell Grant, a federal grant awarded to undergraduates to help pay for their college expenses. Unlike other loans, Pell Grants do not have to be repaid. For Josh, that provided a much-needed lifeline. His caring and involved coach— Shane Smith—never even knew that Josh was ever homeless, otherwise he said that he would have taken him in to live with him!

His running back coach at Mississippi, Greg Knox, helped Josh manage his grant money of approximately $2,100, doling out cash little by little, figuring most eighteen-year-old boys would squander it away on beer, tattoos, and pizza. Not Josh. At the end of the semester, Josh had about $500 left over, and instead of spending the money on himself, he went back home to Mississippi and bought Christmas presents for people he knew were in need. People just like him.

Another young dreamer facing horrendous family circumstances is Jimmy Wayne, or Jimmy Wayne Barber, as he was known before he became a famous country music artist. Like Josh, Jimmy grew up homeless with a mother in jail most of his childhood, and who abused him by completely neglecting and even abandoning him throughout most of his young life. He was also physically abused by his mother's many boyfriends and husbands, and lived hand-to-mouth with his sister, in group homes and foster homes. But he also had a dream to be part of a real family and to someday use his writing and singing talent to make it big in Nashville, Tennessee, or Music City USA, as it is now known. But Jimmy was one of the lucky ones. One day while he was cutting an elderly couple's grass, they invited him into their home and into their lives. Jimmy never left, and thanks to Bea, the mother he never had, he gained the strength and confidence to live the life he was meant to have in the first place. My friend, the author Ken Abraham, along with Jimmy, wrote his life story, which is now a best-selling book called *Walk to Beautiful*, named for Jimmy's walk across the country to raise awareness of childhood homelessness.

My point in telling the inspiring story of Josh Robinson and Jimmy Wayne is to illustrate that dreams can and do come true, as trite as that might sound. They can appear in the darkest of days and to anyone willing to believe in the power of faith and love. Dreams guide us into the light, and without them, we are doomed to darkness. I asked my employees recently, "Will you allow your dreams to lead you to action, participation, and commitment?"

With that in mind, I knew I had dreams of my own. For the first time in my life, I created and owned my own business completely. I had no partners, and because Churchill Mortgage was privately held, it made things simpler in terms of managing a growing enterprise on my own terms and creating a corporate culture based on my vision and belief that family means everything and that all people are valuable and important.

In these more recent years, having Matt at the helm with me made all the difference as well, and I felt so much more comfortable knowing that he would succeed me as CEO when the time came for me to retire. I have been truly blessed to witness our employees buying into our vision, too; this was no easy task given our employee base grew from just a few people to approximately four hundred in 2016.

Actually, my sweet wife, Stephanie, worked for us in the early days of our company. She had a nursing degree and worked in a few medical offices before she went back to college and got her second degree in business. While working at Churchill Mortgage, Stephanie also gained her mortgage lending license by studying and taking the licensing exams. She passed them and actually made the highest grade any of our Churchill Mortgage employees had ever made up to that time, something I am so personally proud of to this day.

When our son, Michael, was born in 2000, she decided it was much more important for our family that she stay home, focusing on making our home an awesome place where Michael felt total support and love. Stephanie also managed most of the daily tasks it takes to just run a great home, such as paying the bills and coordinating the various workers and vendors who help make our home a beautiful and loving place to reside. She said she wanted to be a hands-on mother, and that is one of the reasons I think our youngest son is the incredible young man he is today. Stephanie used her considerable talent and organizational skills to make our home run like a well-oiled machine. It would have been much more difficult for me to handle that on my own while also building and managing a solid and growing company such as Churchill Mortgage. As other CEOs—male or female—know firsthand, having a talented, loving, and involved spouse in your corner can be as valuable an asset as a good balance sheet.

The one thing I could have never predicted was that all four of my children would ever want to be part of Churchill Mortgage. But I'm sure glad they did!

As a father, and as the son of loving and nurturing parents, I have always told my children to dream big and dream often and to follow their own individual paths, regardless if they did or did not coincide with mine.

My oldest daughter, Shayna, went to the University of Tennessee. In her senior year, she married Derek Gunn, and while she got a quality education, she told me that her dream was to become a world-class wife and a world-class mother. She certainly is that and so much more! Shayna married her childhood sweetheart, whose family attended our church.

Derek graduated from UT and went on to obtain his MBA from Georgia State University. I am blessed to have three beautiful grandchildren, Taylor, Harper, and Emerson, as a result of their marriage; I could not be more proud of Shayna.

My other daughter, Megan, ventured up north to Boston University and got her degree in communications and public relations and then moved to New York City to work as a publicist.

Megan has always loved the big cities of New York and Boston. After living and working in New York for several years, she moved to London. Soon thereafter, her boyfriend of five years, Michael Pekhazis, whom she met in college, and Megan tied the knot with a beautiful wedding in the south of France. They continue to live in London. Since January 2011, Megan has worked for Churchill Mortgage taking care of all our internal communications and managing the business relationship with our public relations firm in Atlanta, the G. A. William Mills Agency.

Lawson, who was somewhat of a math whiz in high school, attended Lee University on a math scholarship. I always say that Lawson has that quiet persona but the drive of a lion. He is as competitive and as tough as they come. He came to work at Churchill Mortgage immediately after graduating from college, has been on a solid five-year management training program, and is now preparing to move into the operations management side of our business. I'm also proud to say that on June 24, 2016, he will be a married man. His bride, Cory, is an elementary school teacher with bachelor's and master's Degrees from Middle Tennessee State University.

My youngest son, Michael, is still in high school at Brentwood Academy, and who knows what the future holds for him? He is certainly athletic, playing on the soccer and tennis teams, and he has a very outgoing personality. Michael is a smart and kind young man who never meets a stranger and is full of energy and inquisitiveness. He's also a master of all things technical, like most young people his age; I know he will succeed in anything he does.

But my children's interest in the business caught me by surprise just a few short years ago. First, Lawson came to me and said, "Dad, I want to work for you." I, of course, was elated! Then, Megan called me up one evening at home and was lamenting about her work experience in New York. She was also about to get married and move with her husband to England. "Dad, I was thinking, I really don't want to work for a PR agency anymore and would love to use my communications skills to help you with the business." And the icing on the cake was Shayna; now that her children were in school, she wanted to get involved with Churchill as well. "Dad, I know you are putting together your plan for the company foundation, and I think I can really help you get it off of the ground."

It was a dream come true for me, and I have to be honest in saying that while I knew the pitfalls of bringing family members into the business, I also knew that they could potentially be a huge asset. However, just because they are my kids, I told Matt and my entire management team that they were to be treated no differently than any other Churchill Mortgage employee. We were all relative family members in this business anyway, but just because my children wanted to work here, there would be every expectation that they perform to the best of their abilities and work just a little bit harder to prove that they had the chops.

"My dad is my mentor," Lawson said, "and everything to him becomes a coachable moment. That's just who he is. He surrounds himself with quality people, not toxic ones, and he is a great communicator. We're all a team here, and just because we are his biological family, that doesn't mean we should be treated differently from any other employee. All employees, whether they are family members or not, are treated the same; we are not competitive with each other one bit."

I love hearing Lawson say that because that is the environment I've tried to build in my business life and that directly reflects my personal values as well. In fact, I made sure that Lawson and any of my other kids never ever got special treatment; I made sure our management team knew that too.

Lawson's first job at Churchill was basically one where he started at the bottom, even though he had a great undergraduate business finance degree. The five-year training program began on his first day on the job, where he was assigned to work with our receptionist answering the phones. I had no expectations that he would want to even make a career in the mortgage brokerage industry. I sat back and waited to see if he would take to the business and if there would be career growth in his future. The first morning on the job, I took him aside and told him, "Son, please remember that everyone at Churchill Mortgage, including our receptionist, knows more about the mortgage business than you do. If you really appreciate that, then you will listen a lot and talk a little. You will treat everyone at the company like they're special, and you will try to learn from everyone. If you are successful in doing this, then most of our wonderful employees will grow to love and appreciate you, and if you don't, then they will grow to believe you think you are privileged and special just because you are my son." Sure enough, the boy really enjoyed the field, but he knew, like everyone else, he needed to stand on his own and prove himself.

I'm proud to say that over the four-plus years he has worked for us, he has moved up the ranks and has worked in many phases of the operation and done so with stellar patience and resolve. Our employees have grown to appreciate Lawson, and they know he feels the same way.

"One of the best things about working here is that I can see my dad anytime and get his advice," said Lawson. "I walk into his office and go over near the window, sit on the ledge, and ask him to help me on a particular issue. I'm not the only one who does that either. Dad has an open-door policy with all of his employees, and that's what I love about this company."

Of course, the challenge you face with having your children working for you is that oftentimes others will not complain about them, for fear of reprisal from the boss. I have told all of my team that that is unacceptable, and they are to be treated just like anyone else. So I was prepared for the worst, knowing that at some point Matt or another senior executive would come into my office telling me that my son or daughters were not up to the job. Luckily for me, that has never happened, and, quite to the contrary, we have managed to integrate our real and business families quite beautifully together.

Lawson has done very, very well, by the way, and his love of the business and his talent have led me to discuss his future with Matt, who agrees that after he is set to retire, Lawson is the right man to succeed him. Like I did with Matt, Lawson often accompanies us to industry conferences, even speaking at a few along the way. Just this past year, Lawson was voted in as secretary for the Nashville Mortgage Bankers Association, and last month was voted in again, this time as treasurer of the association. I am very proud of my namesake as he continues to grow in his career.

Megan has used her considerable talents to help us promote Churchill in all of our local markets across the United States, as well as working hard to produce internal communications to help all of our nonhome office teammates, who live and work as far away as California, still feel connected to Churchill Mortgage's operations teams here at the home office. One way she does this is by producing a beautiful full-color newsletter we call the *Churchill News*. This widely read, bimonthly publication is typically sixteen to twenty pages in length, and highlights the various activities of the home office and branch locations. It also gives our extended Churchill family important information on home mortgages, as well as the Churchill Foundation and our employees' volunteer efforts in the communities where they live and work.

Shayna is hard at work helping to address the goals of our newly created Churchill Foundation, working with our various stakeholders to put a structure on what we know will be a meaningful effort to help those in need in our community. We have developed an advisory board comprised of about twelve Churchill Mortgage employees that Shayna works with to help make sure we are actively working to address needs that our employees see and in which they want to get involved. In fact, I am proud that all three are involved in various capacities in our

Churchill Foundation, and we have set the foundation up so that Michael will be involved once he is eighteen years old.

"What I most admire about working with Dad is that he never gets stressed or freaked out about things that happen on a daily basis. He is not a person who panics easily, but a person with a steady hand and a big heart," said Megan. Shayna echoes that thought. "Dad really cares about people and his employees' well-being. He's even-keeled and levelheaded, and when he hires people, he expects transparency, honesty, and loyalty."

As I mentioned before, one of the literal and symbolic ways we encourage and foster that family feeling in the workplace is by our Broomsweeper Award. I decided years ago to take Mr. J. C. Bradford's mantra to his own employees and put a slight twist on it. The original idea of the broomsweeper is that if any employee sees another employee in need of a helping hand, he or she can help that person by figuratively *sweeping* up after the person, helping and assisting wherever he or she sees a need in the company. So in 1998 I started a yearly award, which we called the Broomsweeper Award. Every year since then, we have asked all of our employees to vote on who the ultimate winner will be; I do not have a vote in this process. But what I do is send an e-mail to our employees early in December asking them to consider a few factors in their vote such as: who would they most hate to see leave Churchill; who has the best attitude; who always seems to have a smile on his or her face; and who goes above and beyond in trying to help other employees. I also challenge them to think about other acts of kindness that they have witnessed as well.

In those early days of the award, I asked Teresa Smith, who has been working with us here at Churchill Mortgage for almost two decades, to go to the hardware store and purchase a large natural-bristle broom and to then artfully decorate it. She found some gold leaf paint and covered the entire handle, making it glow and really stand out. Then she bought small metal plates that could be engraved, and her idea was to put the name of the winner on the plate each year and attach it to the handle

117

of the broom, and the employee who won could keep the broom in his or her office for one year so that others will be able to visually see and remember the winner throughout the year.

We take the award seriously, too, recognizing the Broomsweeper Award winner at our annual Christmas dinner party with great fanfare. The lucky employee winner gets to go on a one-week, all-expense-paid trip for two to Hawaii. Believe me, this is something we talk about often throughout the year trying to remind everyone to really live up to the ideals of what the Broomsweeper Award embodies. To my absolute delight, over the seventeen or so years that we've been presenting this award, we have had hundreds of employees step up to the plate helping others both in an out of the office. It might not be as fancy or nationally recognized as the Academy Awards or Tony Awards, but it is Churchill Mortgage's version of the Oscar! Our employees really love it, too.

We also like to reward our Churchill family with what I call unexpected and random acts of kindness. We surprise our employees through a variety of ways, such as giving them flowers, candy, theater tickets, car washes, shoe shine days, pizza days, and a host of other things for no apparent reason other than to say thanks to them for being part of our Churchill family. We have also been known to send flowers to many of the spouses of our employees just to say thank-you to them, too, for their support. It has become a cultural tradition, and I'm pleased to say that our branch managers across the country have done the same thing with their own local employees and their families.

One day I was reading the Bible, as I do most mornings, and I realized that after twenty-three years at the helm of Churchill Mortgage, I needed to think about my own future, my own dreams of life after my career. The business was highly regarded in our industry, we were doing well financially, and I had a strong and dedicated management team in place. We were truly one big happy family! I was also thinking that one of the dreams I realized in my life is to achieve financial security. I have exceeded even my wildest expectations on that front, and wanted my loyal and dedicated family of employees to do the same. What could

I do other than what I've already done to help them achieve that dream and give them a piece of the rock, themselves?

I began researching a tool with which I was vaguely familiar, but hadn't considered years ago as I was building the business. It is called an ESOP—employee stock ownership plan. An ESOP is a way for employees to own stock in a company at no financial cost to them, but rather the shares are awarded based on the mere fact that they are full-time employees. Shares of the company stock are allocated to them annually and are held in a trust until the employee retires, leaves the company, dies, or until the company is sold. I wanted to offer this to our employees to show them how serious I was about being part of the Churchill family and to also encourage productivity and teamwork.

While this is a very cursory summary of the ESOP we now have in place, I knew this innovative tool would serve as a further reward to those who had worked hard to make Churchill Mortgage so successful over the years, as well as being a good recruiting and retention tool. While it is not a great get-rich-quick type of plan, it is a potentially solid tool to help our employees at some point in future years retire in a much better financial condition. As I told our employees the day we announced the ESOP to a standing ovation, "Assuming we all continue to work hard and have as much relative growth as we have experienced in our first two decades, it is highly likely that your stock in our company will be worth more that you could have imagined. Now, keep chopping wood!"

After I launched the program, I was so touched by the many e-mails, cards, and words of kindness that my Churchill family had given to me. What a blessing for sure. And there was one seminal moment for me, too, that happened a couple of years ago that illustrates how we as a team have grown to not only respect one another but love each other, too.

One of the many different leadership activities we do periodically is this: we choose a book on leadership and ask the author to come to our office and talk about the book with our team, and then our employees have a chance to ask the author questions. We usually do these book reviews on Wednesday mornings over a three-or four-week period of time, and each Wednesday morning session usually lasts for an hour or so. Our goal in this effort is to help our management employees grow professionally and, at the same time, think about what they can do to manage their respective teams better, as well as be better human beings in general.

I like to sit in the back of the room during these sessions and quietly observe. I sometimes have to restrain myself from getting involved at all because I do enjoy participating and offering my own thoughts, but I also know I have a tendency to speak up too much. But the real reason for doing these sessions in the first place is to engage our other managers in thoughtful discussions and help them grow.

Two years ago I brought in Cecil Kemp, an author, former owner of a very successful financial planning firm, a CPA by trade, and one of the youngest managers that the former accounting firm Ernst & Young ever hired. He is a solid speaker and life coach, and he really gets into our program, asking employees to read certain chapters of his book in advance and then peppering them with questions that relate to each of the chapters they read.

One of my mangers, Dan Jones, was in the session. Dan started at Churchill as a young man right out of school and was very green. He was an eager beaver, and in those early years I could see that he had real potential. Over his twelve-plus-year career at Churchill, I have enjoyed watching Dan grow into a seasoned professional. While at Churchill, he met his soul mate and got married, had four children, and became a man of great talent, faith, and character.

Dan was one of the more vocal participants in the meeting, raising his hand frequently and asking Cecil questions while offering his own thoughts about leadership.

As he was finishing his last point, my eyes started to tear up. I could feel my heart beating in my chest, beating for the pride and appreciation of Dan Jones, someone who was just like family to me. I watched him grow into such a fine person, and I was overwhelmed listening to the insightful questions he asked and the responses he gave. Just then it hit me. I really am a pastor, and my church is called, *Church*ill Mortgage. For more than twenty years, I have helped my employees not just become better at their jobs, but in their lives, too. I have encouraged them to become better parents, people, spouses, and citizens. I thought to myself, *Lord, well done! Thank you for taking me on this journey and allowing me to be used by you in this manner.* And I knew in my heart that when you truly care about others, and try to help them, you are always rewarded, and you always win.

I have been more blessed in my life to give rather than to receive. That's the promise I made to myself many years ago. It is also the promise I made to all of our nearly four hundred employees. It is not just the dream of helping individuals achieve homeownership that keeps me going every day. It is the fulfillment of dreams of every individual, each one being part of something greater than himself or herself. We are truly one family of God.

I slowly wiped my eyes so no one would see my crying like a baby. Yet, I was thankful for the tears, for they were a constant reminder that without family we are without meaningful and purposeful dreams.

The Hardwick family home in Finley, Tennessee

Mom and Dad's wedding anniversary in 1953

Mom and Dad at their wedding with Pop and Grandmother
Carson and Pop and Grandmother Hardwick

Grandmother and Pop Carson

Mike taking his Grandfather Hardwick on a motorcycle ride

Pop and Grandmother Hardwick at the dedication
of Christ Church's new sanctuary in 1977

Mike in piano concert in 1959

Barney, Montelle, Steve and Mike

Lawson is one cool dude!

Mike's daughters, Shayna and Megan

Mike's long-time mentor and friend, Dick Freeman

Gateway College Quartet with Mike and his cousin Jack Wallace

Michael, Shayna, Poppy, Mike, Megan and Lawson Hardwick
at Dad's 21st birthday party; Dad is a leap-year baby.

Megan and Mike at dinner in La Celle, France in 2014, preparing for Megan's wedding.

Mike, Stephanie and Michael at Megan and Mish's wedding in Provence, France in September, 2014

Matt and Mike presenting Liliana Nigrelli, Churchill's vice president of compliance, with the company's 2015 "Broomsweeper Award."

Mike celebrates Churchill's 24th anniversary with longtime Churchill employees Gina Smith Adams and Kathy Cook.

Mike celebrates Churchill's 24th anniversary with longtime Churchill employee Stephanie Christian

Mike, Dad, Stephanie and Carol in Italy

Sharon and Dave Ramsey with Dad and Carol at Dad's wedding

Mike and Stephanie at home with friends—Sharon and Dave Ramsey,
Tom Black, John & Joan Rich, and Brad Thor & Trish Palmer

Mike and Michael at home in Nashville

Dad and Carol

Mike and Stephanie at Neyland Stadium in Knoxville, Tennessee

Mike's muse, Mike Ballard

Dad with Dr. Billy Graham and friends

Michael and Mike's grandchildren Harper, Taylor and Emerson Gunn

Lawson and Cory Hardwick

Sean Shafer (Mish's best friend), Lawson, Nicole (Mish's sister), Derek and Shayna celebrate Megan and Mish's wedding in France

The happy couple—Megan and Mish

Churchill employees attend the annual CMC
Managers Retreat with Coach Michael Burt

Churchill employees at the company headquarters in Brentwood, TN enjoying the annual Thanksgiving luncheon

Mike and Matt with CMC's top producer, Michael Brown

Lawson sitting on the window sill in Mike's office

Gina Adams, Matt Clarke, Stephanie Christian, Kathy Cook,
Joshua Phillips, Teresa Smith – all longtime CMC employees!

The Hardwick/Carson family Thanksgiving celebration in 2015

Mike, Dad and Steve at Christ Church on Father's Day

Dad doing what he does best

Dad playing his bass

Dad with his boys, grandchildren and great-grandchildren

Mike hanging out in the Titan Stadium with Ronnie
Barrett, Don Scurlock, Dave Ramsey, Larry Gaitlin,
William Lee Golden, TG Sheppard and John Rich

Shayna and Derek Gunn and their children Emerson, Taylor and Harper

Stephanie's sister, Debbie, and her husband,
Elkanah, with their four daughters

Mike at home in Nashville

Megan and Mish at Hardwick Hall in England

Dad and Mom's wedding in 1949

Stephanie and Mike

Churchill Mortgage corporate headquarters in Brentwood, TN.

Mom and Dad

Mike speaking at Churchill's 20th anniversary at the
Nashville Schemerhorn Symphony Hall

Stephanie with her sons, Austin and Michael

Mike presenting a check to The Boot Campaign for Veterans

Mike and Matt with country music star, Josh Turner, at
the 2014 Churchill Mortgage Christmas party

Mike, Lawson, Jim McQuaig and Matt Clarke
at The Masters Golf Tournament

Mike's Antioch High School baseball team.
Mike is in front row, fifth from left

Mike, Michael and Andrew at Kiawah Island

Mike and Stephanie on vacation in Punta Cana, Dominican Republic

Jim McQuaig, Dean Jackson, Joe Stumpf and Mike
Hardwick on a golf trip in Scotland

Stephanie and Taylor at a Nashville Predators hockey game

Churchill asks employees to wear red shirts every Friday to support veterans. Red signifies "Remembering Everyone Deployed"

Mike's family featured on the cover of Brentwood Living Magazine

Mike and Stephanie on vacation with Dave and
Sharon Ramsey in the Cayman Islands

The Hardwick family circa 1955

Matt, Mike and Jim McQuaig playing golf at Bandon Dunes, Oregon

Mike and Stephanie with Bob and Mary Clement in France

Dad with Billy Graham, Michael W. Smith and other notable
pastors and businessmen from Middle Tennessee

Churchill Mortgage Annual Managers Retreat during
a team building exercise at Pursell Farms

Stephanie and Sharon Ramsey at a UT football game

Mike and Megan at Megan's wedding

Stephanie and her brother Bo and sister Debbie

Stephanie with friends during a 2016 trip in Israel

Stephanie's parents, Jim and Jewel Buford

Matt Clarke

Family ski trip at Deer Valley with Pastor & Carol
Hardwick and Stephanie and Mike

Churchill employees raising money for Leukemia and Lymphoma Society

Mike reading the Christmas Story to his grandchildren

Mike and Lawson relaxing in Turks and Caicos

The boss gets dunked at a CMC employee summer picnic party

Churchill employees supporting Second Harvest Food Bank

The churches that Dad built

Dad

Franklin National Bank (FNB) in Franklin, Tennessee

Franklin National Bank in Franklin, Tennessee

Gordon Inman, Franklin National Bank Chairman,
on the day when FNB went public

Uncle Joe Carson

Sony and Dean Jackson, Steve & Polly, Bob Clement and
Stephanie and Mike on vacation in Cabo, Mexico

Mike, Stephanie and John Maxwell

Dad, Stephanie and Mike with a portrait of
Montelle Hardwick at Christ Church

Dad in his Cohn High School band uniform as the Drum Major

Mike & Stephanie Hardwick

Uncle Jim Hardwick with wife Aileen and granddaughters

Mike with Jim McQuaig golfing in Palm Springs, California

Mike dancing with granddaughters Emerson and Harper

Dad, Carol, Stephanie, Mike, Steve and Polly in England

Steve, Mike, Mish, Dad and Mish's dad, Fadoul at his home in London

Derek, Shayna, Steve, Polly, Stephanie and Mike in Jerusalem

Stephanie's daughter, Alex

Gary and Delilah Gunn with Dave and Sharon Ramsey

CHAPTER 10

The Triumphs and Pitfalls of
Being an Entrepreneur

I can accept failure. Everyone fails at something. But I cannot accept not trying.—Michael Jordan

Life is a journey; there is no question about that. But when it comes to business, it is a trip that needs to be carefully planned, realizing that there will always be pitfalls along the way. Despite filling the car up with gas, meticulously going over GPS maps to make sure the best route is chosen, and packing enough sandwiches and cookies for the kids, still things can and will go wrong. There will always be that pesky nail in the road that will deflate a tire, taking a wrong turn due to the GPS not being up-to-date that will add hours to the trip, or forgetting to bring knives to spread mustard on the turkey sandwiches; that's just how it goes.

Being an entrepreneur taps into the adventurer in all of us, and for those who are willing to embrace that inner road warrior, it can be an electrifying way to make a living. For some reason, I have always loved being an entrepreneur. I loved creating things, starting new businesses, and being out on a limb, so to speak. It takes lots of planning, perseverance, fluidity, faith, flexibility, and the confidence to never give up, and to simply keep chopping wood, as I've often said. Former First Lady Barbara Bush, one great woman I certainly admire, said something that I think aptly applies to the spirit of an entrepreneur:

"You don't luck into things as much as you'd like to do. You build step by step, whether it's friendships or opportunities." Just as Coach Butch Jones of my beloved Tennessee Volunteers said, "The key to building a winning football team is by doing it brick by brick," meaning slowly and carefully with intention and dogged effort.

I believe that, in an ironic way, we are all in business for ourselves, whether someone is the owner of a company, a head football coach, or an employee working for someone else. By that I mean that if you are an employee, you either do a good job or you risk losing that job. Some people often mistakenly believe that business owners are immune from feeling the pain of losing, but that couldn't be further from the truth. If I don't do a good job, I risk our business failing. At the end of the day, that means I don't have any income, plus I probably lost everything I put into starting up the business, as well as being part of the reason many employees lose their jobs and incomes.

I think that the reason most new businesses don't survive their first five to ten years is that so many business owners don't anticipate or plan for the ups and downs that will inevitably take place. Take it from me, I know what it is like to lose everything, and it is not fun! I have felt the pain of failure, worrying how I was going to pay the bills and put food on the table. And as an entrepreneur, I am harder on myself than I am with any of my employees. But over the years, I have learned that failure does not have to define a person. And it can be overcome by following some steps that I have found to work for me and that other business entrepreneurs have practiced successfully over the years, too.

Another one of my sports heroes, Babe Ruth, was well known as the home-run king for several decades. But not many people realize he was also one of the leading strikeout guys. For many years, Babe Ruth was known as the king of strikeouts, and for his all-or-nothing batting style. He led the American League in strikeouts five times and fanned 1,330 times in his career. In fact, old Babe actually struck out almost twice as many times as he hit home runs. Being a successful entrepreneur means experiencing the pitfalls of owning a business, but also the triumph of occasionally hitting home runs out of the park.

Here is a great story about one of my closest friends and fellow entrepreneurs, Dave Ramsey. He is one of the most well-respected personal finance gurus in the country, with many *New York Times* bestselling books under his belt, a nationally syndicated radio show that is consistently ranked in the top three in the country, and a thriving consulting business. Dave can literally light up a room with his giant smile, tremendous enthusiasm, and even greater heart; he's the kind of person others just can't get enough of. As the author Paul Marston has said, and I agree: "Excellence is not a skill; it is an attitude." And Dave's attitude is excellent.

While Dave and I grew up almost literally next door to each other, and we both attended Haywood Elementary School and Antioch High School on the south side of Nashville, I actually got to really know Dave personally several years later when he graduated from the University of Tennessee, married his college sweetheart, Sharon, and moved back to Nashville. At that particular time, Dave and Sharon had two young daughters, Denise and Rachel, and had just started attending Christ Church, where my father was the pastor. I was teaching a young married couples' class at the church, and Dave and Sharon were often attendees. It was obvious to me that Dave and I had so much in common. We were both young married men with small daughters, had achieved a significant level of success in the real estate and finance business, and the two of us got caught up in the whirlwind of the infamous Tax Reform Act of 1986. As most listeners of Dave's radio show know, Dave went through personal bankruptcy; I avoided it, but ever so narrowly!

Dave and I soon became fast friends, and in those days we would often get together to share our sad tales of financial failure and loss. There were many times when we would even argue over who would be the one to pay for the cheap Krystal Burgers, since neither of us could afford anything more! (I would say that Krystal Burgers would be comparable to a White Castle or Sonic burger—no offense to either of those enterprises, as at times I just couldn't resist their mouth-watering lure.) Our lunch get-togethers were sometimes pity parties too, where one or both of us would decry how bad things had gotten and wonder just how we were going to get through and start all over again.

It was at one of those lunch meetings, shortly after I had enjoyed the success of helping start and run Franklin National Bank and then Churchill Mortgage, that Dave dropped an idea by me that he had been pondering for some time. Namely, he wanted to start a talk radio show dealing with how to properly handle, of all things, money! Though that was so many years ago, I recall literally laughing out loud, and telling Dave what a bad idea I thought it was. I remember saying to him, "Why would anyone listen to you, buddy, since you have just come out of bankruptcy!" Well, if you know Dave Ramsey at all, then you know he is not someone who makes any decision lightly. And, once he does make up his mind, he is not the type of person who can easily be talked out of it either. Without a second of hesitation, Dave told me in no uncertain terms, "Mike, they *will* listen because I can tell them what *not* to do with their money!" Well, I had no clever comeback to that comment, so I had to quickly come up with another idea to hopefully change his mind. No matter what his rationale, I truly didn't believe this would be a successful business venture.

Dave explained to me that he had found a bankrupt radio station in Manchester, Tennessee, that had agreed to sell him airtime for a relatively small amount of money, and he was looking for a good advertiser, which was why he was talking with me. Clearly he wasn't just seeking my advice, but rather he wanted me to come on board as an advertiser! Seriously, I didn't see this as something that would work, so I tried once again to talk him out of it. "Dave," I said, "there is a reason why that radio station went bankrupt, because nobody was listening to it." I further explained to him that since our families lived well over an hour away from Manchester, Tennessee, they would not even be able to hear his show or any of my advertisements. So what was the point? In fact, I seem to recall that station was only a ten-thousand-watt station, and its antenna was only operating at half power at that.

Well, Dave, being the great salesperson that he was, quickly replied rather convincingly, "Mike, the cost to get the show up and running is not really that much at all. Plus, I can test and practice my radio show hosting skills to a small audience before I could ever hope to go with a bigger station in a much larger market." To my surprise, that made a lot of sense to me, and, besides, Dave is a very hard guy to say no to. So I acquiesced and agreed to become his first radio sponsor. Boy, am I ever glad I made that decision!

Today, *The Dave Ramsey Show* is rated number two or three in the entire country, depending on what rating service is doing the calculation. The only other radio show that is consistently rated number one is Rush Limbaugh's. Dave's show is broadcast in all fifty states and on more than 530 radio stations, and he has at least nine million loyal daily listeners. Because of our support of his show as an advertiser, today, Churchill Mortgage receives thousands of new calls each and every month from Dave's audience asking us to help them achieve the American dream of homeownership. I would say that is a pretty good return on investment! I often pray and thank God that Dave didn't listen to me during our lunch meetings when all either of us could afford was that Krystal hamburger.

Dave is a great example of how successful entrepreneurs weather the ups and downs of business ownership and, regardless of the challenges, continue to pursue their vision and never give up.

Another one of my business heroes is Jack Canfield, a motivational speaker and cocreator of *Chicken Soup for the Soul* book series. He once said, "The longer you hang in there, the greater the chance that something will happen in your favor. No matter how hard it seems, the longer you persist, the more likely your success."

Surviving the many pitfalls of owning a business is a skill that I was fortunate to learn early in my career and that helped me realize a very important lesson. That lesson is to not fear failure, but rather view it as a stepping-stone to eventual success. Now don't get me wrong. I don't like to fail at anything. Frankly, I hate to lose! But I have learned that every time I fail at something, if I just get back up and try again and again, eventually I can realize improvement, learn from my failure, and ultimately succeed; at least that is usually the case.

Working for Dick Freeman early in my career taught me so much about running a business and weathering the proverbial slings and arrows along the way. Mr. Freeman and his father and brothers were all well known in the real estate circles of Nashville. Mr. Harvey, Dick Freeman's father, started Harvey Freeman & Sons many years back in the early1950s, and had a very successful business when I first met Dick in the 1980s. Dick was an entrepreneur in every sense of the word. He was not afraid of risk, was highly motivated, was always willing to teach and mentor others, and had a very big and generous nature.

Some of the most important lessons that I learned from Dick and were able to use in starting my own companies included: how to interview potential job applicants, how to treat people who work for you, how to properly do a solid financial analysis on income-producing real estate, how to think through a business opportunity and not allow emotions to get in the way, be willing to walk away if the numbers don't justify the investment, to eradicate the word *failure* from your vocabulary, and, most of all, to never give up! One of many thoughts Dick shared with me was this gem of a comment: "You don't make money when you sell a property, but rather you make money when you purchase a property." By that he simply meant if you don't purchase a property at a fair price, then you will have a very difficult time ever making any meaningful return on your investment when you sell the property. Dick always taught me to never get emotionally involved with a property until *after* I had closed on its purchase; otherwise, I might easily overpay.

This was integral to surviving the financial failure and loss of almost everything when Dick's vast real estate holdings and various real estate companies, including our condo conversion company, went belly-up after the Tax Reform Act of 1986 was fully implemented and the results took effect. It was one of the toughest times in my life without a doubt, and for Dick as well. Actually, by the late 1980s I had built up quite a personal financial statement, and, therefore, had a lot to lose at the time, especially my self-esteem, which was at an all-time low. And it almost did me in, but for my faith in God and the support of my parents and close friends.

Surviving what some would describe as clinical depression for eight months was in hindsight a pivotal moment in my life, and taught me another valuable lesson, and that was to tackle any problem that came my way with strength and determination. Successful entrepreneurs know that these negative blips on the radar can actually be somewhat energizing. They force you to reevaluate your situation and chart new ideas, and they can propel your business in another, more positive, direction.

The experience I had working for Dick Freeman laid the foundation for my being able to play a very significant role in starting both Franklin National Bank and Churchill Mortgage. I have no doubt that without my experience of working for and learning so much from Dick during those years, I would never have been able to even consider starting a bank, let alone think I could build a national mortgage company. Dick helped build in me the ability to believe I could actually do things such as that.

To this day, Dick is like a second father to me, and I always felt so comfortable being around his wife, Mary, his son, Criswell, and his two daughters—Mary Jo and Donna. My children and Dick's grandchildren grew up spending much time together, and Dick and Mary are even referred to in our family as Uncle Dick and Aunt Mary. After forty years of successfully starting and operating four or five different types of businesses with his fathers and brothers, Dick Freeman will always be regarded as one of Nashville's most well-respected and successful entrepreneurs. I can't describe how much I love and appreciate him, for without his mentorship I would have not been able to enjoy the success God has allowed me and my family to enjoy through Franklin National

Bank and Churchill Mortgage Corporation over the past twenty-five to thirty years.

Most everyone has heard of business legends Bill Gates, Walt Disney, Fred Smith, and Thomas Edison. Each has experienced crazy success in business, but folks don't often realize that all four of them also experienced failures at one time or another. Bill Gates, of course, created Microsoft and quickly became enormously successful and wildly rich, yet he was a college dropout. Walt Disney is well-known and beloved internationally, and yet he was fired from a job as a young man. His employer said that Walt was lacking in imagination and any original ideas. Of all things! Fred Smith was the founder of FedEx, headquartered in Memphis, Tennessee. When he was a student at Yale University, he turned in a paper in his economics class where he shared an idea on how to start a mail/parcel service that could deliver packages overnight. Ironically, he received a very low grade! And the great American inventor and businessman Thomas Edison perhaps shared one of the most significant quotes about failure when he stated, "I have not failed. I've just found ten thousand ways that won't work." Not only did he invent the lightbulb and motion picture camera, he was one of the first entrepreneurs to use the principle of mass production. I've taken his words to heart many, many times throughout my life.

While I have always had a strong competitive nature, I learned not to worry that much about failure. Why? Because I started out with very little, knew how to live on little, and knew if I failed, I could just start over again. Don't get me wrong; I never wanted to fail, and was willing to work my proverbial rear end off so I wouldn't totally fail, but I knew from experience that even through the darkest days, the sun will always appear. I recall a line from an old Billy Preston song called "Nothing from Nothing," that goes something like this: "Nothing from nothing leaves nothing." Since I came from nothing financially, I never spent much time thinking what I would do if I lost it all. And, once I actually did almost lose it all, ironically, it gave me the strength to work tirelessly and never let that happen again.

From Dick Freeman, I learned how to be resilient even during the toughest of times, and from another one of my business heroes, Gordon Inman, I learned the art of the deal.

Gordon Inman, who is seventy-seven, as I have mentioned, was the first major investor in Franklin National Bank. He started his career working in a small Shell Gas Station in the working-class section of Nashville called Woodbine, where he was a self-described grease monkey. Then out of the blue he got a call from one of his customers—none other than Dr. Thomas Frist Sr., the physician and future founder of the healthcare giant HCA, as well as the father of Tennessee Senator Bill Frist. As the story goes, the good doctor liked Gordon and thought he had the intellect and drive to go into medicine, which he enthusiastically encouraged him to pursue. But Gordon had other dreams of his own. He wanted to be an entrepreneur and make money. Boy, did he ever!

Gordon, like Steve and I, learned about business by selling things. Gordon sold fruit to his neighbors as a young boy, though I think Steve and I were more fortunate to sell those Krispy Kreme doughnuts. His drive and tenacity really paid off, and Gordon soon got his real estate license and began his road toward becoming a successful banker, real estate mogul, and philanthropist. He also invested in so many interesting enterprises, from our regional bank in Franklin to wireless phone companies, health food ventures, and even hospitality, not just here in Nashville but around the country.

Gordon also had the vision to imagine the possibility that our small regional bank could one day be a big player in the banking industry. He also had a sixth sense when it came to identifying and seizing an opportunity, and he wasn't afraid to take a huge risk, which was evident by his investing such a large amount of money in our new banking venture. Gordon has that special ability to see an opportunity when it arises and knows how to get in and out of businesses like Houdini did out of his restraints! Dick Freeman always told me it's all about, "Timing, timing, timing!" It has been a blessing for me to have learned from my good friend Gordon Inman, whose timing has always seemed to be nearly impeccable.

Another friend of mine, the country music artist, singer songwriter, and fifteen-time Grammy nominee John Rich, who is part of the duo Big & Rich, is a living example of entrepreneurship, albeit it in the music industry. As many people know, being in music, and country music in particular, is a tough road to pursue. Millions of talented artists never make it to the big time, and some who do often get caught in the trap of being managed unscrupulously or of not taking charge of their own finances or futures. John defies that model and, like Taylor Swift, has risen to the top of the country music world with humility yet a big personality, professionalism, and philanthropy.

John knew early on in his career that he had to work hard—keep chopping wood, as I like to say—to get to the point where he honed his performing skills to the degree that audiences would want to pay to hear him sing. He would perform his original songs in small-town bars across his home state of Texas and other venues all across the country to refine his musical chops. He had no problem taking the baby steps needed to become the consummate professional he is today. Even when he was fired from his first band, Lonestar, he never gave up. Instead, he was motivated to embark on a solo career teaming up with Big Kenny in 2003 and releasing three albums, including many number one singles. He has also hosted a reality television show, called *Gone Country*, was a judge on *Nashville Star*, and was a candidate on *Celebrity Apprentice*, and even won the reality show competition, raising more than $1.4 million for charity. Over the years, John has encouraged and supported other emerging artists through his Muzik Mafia, working with them on their performing and composition skills. Building a business, just like a music career, takes a person who is willing to take risks, accept rejection as a means for improvement, and remain positive no matter what life has in store.

By the time Churchill Mortgage was up and running, I had internalized the lessons I had learned from my mentor Dick Freeman and great friend Gordon Inman, as well as my parents, grandparents, and uncles. In fact, my Uncle Alton, who worked for Genesco Inc., a specialty retailer headquartered in Nashville, reputedly made the very first boots that the Beatles wore when they visited America for the first time and appeared on the Ed Sullivan show. Like everyone in my family, being an entrepreneur was something that was just in our DNA.

Still, as everyone who owns a business large or small knows, there are always times when business slows down. When those inevitable times come, you have to be able to continue running your business as a *real* business. By that I mean you have to make some very tough decisions. For example, a few times over the twenty-four years we have been in business, we simply have had to lay some people off. This is never a pleasant experience, and it is certainly not an easy thing to do, either. But, if you don't make those tough decisions and do them in a timely manner, it could put the entire company in grave jeopardy. For entrepreneurs, that can be especially draining. Unlike a CEO of a large, publicly held company, when it is your own business, you feel like you are letting members of your own family down. It's not that CEOs don't care, but as a business owner, I know that if I am wrong about something, ultimately it is on me. Laying people off is as personal as it gets.

I will never forget that awful day. Our industry slowed down to the point that we were taking in less money than we were paying out in expenses, so the only way to reduce our costs for the greater good of the company was to trim the payroll by about twenty-five or so employees. I probably waited a bit too long to do it, and we ran through $1million in cash. It was starting to impact the financial health of Churchill Mortgage. Once I made the gut-wrenching decision to do the layoffs, I knew that I had to execute it with great care and explain why I had to make the call to employees about whom I deeply cared.

I decided to hold an off-site meeting with the folks who I had to terminate and explain to them in depth why I had to make the decision. I sat with them for more than two hours, laying out in detail our entire financial situation. I went meticulously through all of our numbers and showed them where the company was and what we were facing. I explained that they were all good people, wonderful employees, and even better friends, and that they had nothing whatsoever to do with the company's financial dilemma. The market conditions were solely to blame, and I wanted them to know how much I valued them. We all cried at the end of that meeting, but I promised that someday when we were in better shape, I would be calling them to come back to work for me.

Over the years I have tried to instill in all of our employees and my children the value of money—how to wisely appreciate it and, therefore, properly handle it, too. And I am happy to say that about a year after that layoff, I was able to get in touch with most of those affected employees and welcome many of them back to Churchill with open arms.

One of the more recent traditions now incorporated into our Churchill Mortgage culture is the Friday Morning Message, an e-mail blast that we created to help motivate our employees. Every Friday one of our talented employees, such as John Lann, sends an e-mail companywide that has a motivational message ending a productive week on a positive note. I thought this one recently sent by John illustrates how someone can overcome obstacles and succeed in ways they never thought possible. Here is John's Friday Morning Message:

> High school wasn't easy for Bill. He wanted to fit in; he wanted to make friends, and he desperately wanted to play sports. Unfortunately, at that age, he didn't have an athletic bone in his body. He was taller than most, lanky, awkward, and highly uncoordinated. But that didn't deter Bill from following his dream of playing sports. As a tenth-grader, he decided to try out for the junior varsity basketball team. The number of roster spots on the team was limited, and it seemed as if the entire tenth grade tried out for the team. So, the coach had no choice but to deliberately trim the roster. He told the kids that after each practice, he would post a list of players that would

advance to the next tryout. After the very first practice, Bill ran to the bulletin board to look for his name. No matter how many times he read it, he couldn't find his name. Bill was devastated, heart-broken, and embarrassed. After just one tryout, Bill was cut from the team—his dreams shot down forever. At least that's what he thought until a gentleman put his hand on his shoulder.

The hand belonged to George Powles, the varsity basketball coach. He had been watching the JV tryouts and saw a hidden talent in this young man. That's why George said that being cut from the JV team wasn't the end of the world. In fact, it was a good thing, because he wanted Bill to try out for the varsity team! Bill said, "But I just got cut from the JV team!" George explained that the only thing Bill needed was experience. He simply needed to play basketball every day. So George drove Bill to the local Boys & Girls Club, took two dollars from his pocket and paid for his membership.

Playing every day after school paid off. With George as his mentor, Bill made the varsity team as a junior. He wasn't an outstanding player, but you could see his potential. While in high school, Bill also experienced a growth spurt. He grew four inches taller and was the tallest player on the team. By his senior year, Bill was accomplished enough to earn a scholarship at the University of San Francisco, where he blossomed. In college, Bill continued to grow physically and mentally. His height was soon measured at six feet ten tall, and he was one of the smartest players on the court. He was becoming a basketball star. In fact, Bill led the San Francisco Dons to fifty-six consecutive victories and back to back NCAA championships.

The young man who was embarrassingly cut after his first junior varsity practice went on to fulfill his dream of being a professional athlete. The Boston Celtics drafted Bill, and he subsequently led them to eleven NBA championships, with an unprecedented eight in a row! Did I mention Bill was also a five-time MVP as well? Bill will tell you today that if it weren't for the kindness, support and vision of George Powles, he would not have pursued basketball. Mentors are difference makers. Mentors change the lives of men and women every day. As Bill says, "None of us made it on our own."

By the way, Bill's full name is: William Felton Russell. You know him better as Bill Russell.

January is National Mentoring Month, and Bill Russell urges you to accept the call of mentorship. He challenges you to pay it forward and make a positive difference in someone's life, just as George Powles did for him.

Make it a productive day, and keep chopping wood!"

John's Friday Morning Message certainly did inspire me! Every Friday when I read John's latest message, I am motivated to give just a little more, to really focus on being better that day and becoming the successful business person I aspire to be.

The bottom line is this: to be a successful entrepreneur, in my opinion, one must study the strengths and weaknesses of others who have taken the same path, and not be afraid to take a risk. My father took a risk—building his first small church with his own hands and growing it to a membership of over eight thousand people. Dick Freeman took a risk by hiring me and starting a condo-conversion company—one of just a few in the country at the time—and expanding it regionally. Dave Ramsay used his financial failure to advise others how to handle money and created his own nationally syndicated radio show. Gordon Inman went from pumping gas and working on cars, to owning some of the most profitable businesses in multiple industries throughout the United States. John Rich began his career singing in honky-tonk bars to becoming one of the biggest stars in country music today, and Bill Russell never gave up on his dream of playing professional basketball.

These successful people have much in common. That is, the ability to pay attention to detail, not fear of hard work and willingness to put in very long hours, unwavering discipline, the willingness to listen and learn from others, tackling a problem with vigor and determination, working well with others, having a positive attitude, recognizing the needs of others and offering assistance, highly valuing the contributions of others, the willingness to teach and mentor, and never fearing failure, but rather viewing it as a stepping-stone of success. I am sure that each of them could quickly cite other risks they took that didn't work out so well, but that did not keep them from trying over and over again.

There are surely some pitfalls to being an entrepreneur. But the triumphs are almost always worth the investment if the entrepreneur carefully and dutifully prepares for the journey.

CHAPTER 11

My Personal Rushmore:
Reagan and Churchill

If we ever forget that we are One Nation under God, then we will be a nation gone under.—Ronald Reagan

On October 31, 1941, after fourteen years of chipping away into the rugged granite of Mount Rushmore in South Dakota, four American presidents' images were preserved for eternity. Thomas Jefferson, George Washington, Theodore Roosevelt, and Abraham Lincoln now grace the majestic mountain, in what today is a popular tourist destination, attracting more than three million visitors every year.

Even though it took more than four hundred men working in often harsh and inclement conditions to complete the project, remarkably no one ever died. I have always been amazed that their sixty-foot-high faces were carved using blasts from dynamite and then artfully chiseled with jackhammers and refined by hand. These dedicated workers kept chopping granite, and, like so many other great men and women who have achieved to their highest potential, they "kept chopping wood" and never gave up!

When I had the good fortune to visit the memorial several years ago, I stood gazing up at the images of these inspirational leaders of our great nation, and I thought about what they did to achieve greatness, not to mention their faces preserved for eternity on the side of a mountain. They each had different personalities, family backgrounds, financial status, and physical appearances. But their common denominator, in my opinion, is their love of country, faith in God, and belief in something greater than themselves.

Though their images are not carved in granite, Ronald Reagan and Winston Churchill have nevertheless made their mark on our world and have been my personal Mount Rushmore ever since I became an adult.

Winston Churchill once said, "Courage is what it takes to stand up and speak. Courage is also what it takes to sit down and listen." No truer words have ever been said, and, in fact, Churchill has said so many memorable things that I would be hard-pressed to name them all.

Sir Winston Churchill was the quintessential Renaissance man. A British statesman who served as prime minister twice, leader of the Conservative Party, minister of defense, first lord of the admiralty, among other notable positions, he is considered among the greatest wartime leaders of the twentieth century. Churchill was also a historian, a novelist, and an artist. He even won the Nobel Prize in literature in 1953, and he was also the first person ever to become an honorary citizen of the United States.

His sense of decency and integrity were fully on display when he was among the first to warn against the evils of Nazi Germany and its tyrannical leader, Adolf Hitler. After being out of politics, once World War II commenced, he replaced Neville Chamberlain and once again became prime minister. He had no intention of letting his country fall to the Nazis. He took to the airwaves to deliver rousing speeches encouraging the British people to reject Adolf Hitler and spurred the British Resistance until finally the Nazis were defeated. He was brilliant, passionate, multifaceted, and a great communicator.

Everything Churchill did during his remarkable career took great courage and tenacity. He fully exhibited a never-quit attitude and approach to life. He was very determined, too, and his belief in freedom and his love of country knew no bounds. Even after the war was over, he was a powerful voice for warning his country about the threat of the Soviet Union, as well as other threats. But Churchill was also a man who deeply cared about the health and welfare of people, and during his second term as prime minister, focused on building Great Britain back up again and introducing health and safety practices in the workplace as well as new safety regulations for housing and development.

Now, a few folks might consider the following analogy between Winston Churchill and Lloyd Christmas, the name of the character Jim Carey played in the movie *Dumb and Dumber* a bit unusual. But I have used it often with my employees, and it illustrates that never-give-up attitude that both Churchill and Christmas embodied, though, of course, with very different motivations!

In the 1994 movie, Lloyd Christmas, who was a limousine driver, and I dare say not the brightest bulb in the shed, fell madly in love with a woman played by Lauren Holly, who he had never met when she stepped into his limo for a ride to the airport. He was immediately infatuated with her charm and beauty but didn't have the courage to ask her out for a date while he was driving her to the airport. After she got out of the limo, he helped her bring her bags into the terminal, and after she boarded the plane to Aspen, Colorado, he realized she left a briefcase full of money behind. He didn't know at the time that she did this purposely to provide ransom money for her kidnapped husband. This began a nationwide search from Providence to Aspen with his sidekick—Harry Dunne, played by Jeff Daniels—to find her and return her case. He and Harry drove clear across America, all the while Christmas was fantasizing about the life they might have together.

Finally, he tracked her down at a fund-raiser held in a luxury five-star hotel, and was thrilled to be able to see his love object again and be the shining knight in armor who saved her from financial ruin by delivering her precious briefcase. So here is how Christmas handled the situation, and the main lesson learned from this engaging story: Christmas said to Mary, getting his words totally mixed up, "I can't tell you how crazy I am about you, Mary. What are the chances that a girl like me could get a boy like you?"

"Lloyd, I really don't think so," she said.

"Well, let me ask you this," he said. "Come on, Mary, hit me with it. What are my odds?"

"One in million," she replied. "So, Mary, what you are telling me is that I have a chance?"

Lloyd Christmas was always looking for that next opportunity and, like Churchill, never gave up or took no for an answer.

I think that Sir Winston Churchill is the embodiment of the qualities a transformational leader should possess. Here's why: any person who desires to lead others has to have a wide range of interests. Certainly Churchill did. Think about that for a moment. If someone is leading a company or a government with more than one person, and, of course, that is always the case, then that leader will have to adapt to dealing with many different personalities, skill sets, interests, and talents. If a leader has too narrow a world view, or exhibits too narrow of a skill set himself or herself, how could that person possibly relate to others? How could he or she have the emotional intelligence and empathy to lead effectively? As Winston Churchill so eloquently said in this famous quote: "We make a living by what we get, but we make a life by what we give."

Another of Churchill's considerable gifts was his ability to influence people and change hearts and minds. I could hold all the advanced degrees in the world and have the highest IQ score, but none of that matters if I fail to engage others, and, as the biblical admonition in Philippians 2:3 suggests, "Esteem others more highly than yourself."

Remembering Churchill's lessons in tenacity and resolve helped me though some of the toughest times in my own life especially when I was battling depression. With the help of God and my incredible family, as well as many wonderfully caring friends, I began to realize that I, indeed, could come back. I knew things wouldn't be easy, but I learned that my failure was not going to defeat me. I didn't quit. I didn't walk away. I didn't try to cover up my financial failure.

While Churchill's face is not carved in the side of a mountain, I want to thank Sir Winston for giving me a small part of his wisdom and insights.

Even though Ronald Reagan did not come from great wealth and privilege like Winston Churchill, in my opinion, they shared many of the same personality traits, and each in his own way was able to motivate and inspire people from all walks of life. I have always admired him, not so much as simply a transformational president, but a remarkable cheerleader-in-chief!

Historians are divided as to whether Reagan was a "great" president, defining greatness in the presidency as someone who has made permanent changes in society such as Franklin D. Roosevelt did with Social Security or Lyndon B. Johnson with Medicare and civil rights. But Ronald Reagan had that special something—a quality that regardless of his lasting political achievements has made him unforgettable. That is, his ability to communicate in a way that captivated his audience and brought the country together through positive and inspirational messaging. His ability to help Americans begin to believe in our country again single-handedly helped turn the Carter years of lethargy back to some of the greatest years in our democracy, at least in my opinion. That is the essence of true leadership.

Clearly, the fortieth president of the United States' boyhood years were not spent being chauffeured to and from a private school by his nanny. To the contrary, he came from quite poor circumstances, growing up in small towns in northern Illinois. He was born in a very tiny apartment in a commercial building in Tampico, moved frequently, then finally settled back in Tampico and again lived in another commercial building—this one the H. C. Pitney Variety Store. My family didn't have great wealth, either, but we had stability in terms of living in only a few homes in a small town in the South where everyone looked out for each other.

But despite Reagan's lack of material wealth, somehow he never let that define him. In fact, he seemed to defy the odds and retained the belief that people are essentially good at heart; he seemed to care deeply for all of them. Many have said that his belief in God and the faith of his mother influenced him tremendously during his youth and set the stage for his kind and gentle demeanor as an adult. It just goes to show that when parents surround their children with love and faith, they can truly overcome many of life's unforeseen challenges.

When Ronald Reagan was in college, it was said he was an average student but was known as someone who could do many things fairly well such as sports, theater, and even student government. Being well-rounded and curious is something I have observed over the years as qualities of successful leaders; again, my good friend Gordon Inman is a great example of that.

Always curious and involved, Reagan's career went from acting to politics, Democrat to Republican, governor to president, and now someone who is revered worldwide, and I would dare say in some circles, even canonized.

But why was this? At a 2015 Heritage Foundation Symposium on Ronald Reagan, historians and academics shared some very interesting and often divergent views about his legacy. And, of course, there are countless biographies written about him as well, some of which I've read and have always found fascinating. One of the symposium panelists, the historian Stephen Ambrose, said, "Reagan will be remembered as the president who reversed the decades-old flow of power to Washington." I would add that he also: reduced the unemployment rate from 7.5 percent to 5.25 percent, survived almost being assassinated, signed the Tax Reform Act of 1986, told Mikhail Gorbachev to "tear down this wall," appointed the first woman to the Supreme Court, and gave the country hope once again.

Another member of the Heritage Foundation panel, professor Alonzo L. Hamby of Ohio University, said about Reagan and I agree: "Reagan has been an up-lifter and rhetorician comparable to the two Roosevelts and Wilson; a conservative exponent of capitalism in the tradition of Coolidge and Eisenhower; a cold warrior and advocate of US international leadership akin to Truman, Kennedy and Nixon. These analogies demonstrate the skill and strength of a political leader able to draw on diverse themes and weave them together into a formidable personal coalition."

This was a fascinating transcript for me to read for so many reasons. But, regardless of the success or failure of Reagan's policies and programs, in the hearts and minds of most Americans, he is still remembered as a great leader. In fact, I'm reminded of a quote by Harry Truman that illustrates this very well: "In reading the lives of great men, I found that the first victory they won was over themselves; self-discipline with all of them came first."

In reading about the lives of so many great leaders, I am convinced that Ronald Reagan is so highly valued and remembered because he was simply a superb communicator, and, much like Sir Winston Churchill, he never allowed his defeats to stop him or cause him to give up. Regardless of one's political persuasion, even some of his detractors could still admire him for his earnest approach to politics and his ability to forge relationships with folks who did not share his beliefs. I've always been struck by that quality in him. He had such a cordial and friendly working relationship with Former US House Speaker Tip O'Neill—two men who were completely at odds politically. He also became great friends with Prime Minister Margaret Thatcher, and he found ways to work with all of them, regardless of what political side of the aisle they were from.

That gets back to my point about putting others first. Many of my employees and I share different ideas and points of view, but at the end of the day it is all about respect, reasonable and responsible compromise, and focusing on the big picture. Ronald Reagan said it best himself: "There are no constraints on the human mind, no walls around the human spirit, and no barriers to our progress except those we ourselves erect."

Dick Freeman also taught me a great lesson in that regard. One day many years ago, Dick invited me to lunch, as he often did. When I arrived that afternoon in his beautifully decorated downtown Nashville office, he walked me into his large conference room, where he had brought in box lunches for us to enjoy while we had our meeting. He asked me to sit in the end seat at the conference table, a chair that was always reserved for him. I initially hesitated, telling him, "Mr. Freeman, that is your seat; I would be more than happy to sit at a side chair." He insisted, so I acquiesced and pulled out "his" chair as he requested. After a few minutes of talking pleasantries and eating our lunch, Dick mentioned that he wanted to discuss something that he felt strongly about and which he knew could be beneficial to me. "Mike, I want you to listen to my heart in what I'm about to tell you. If you only hear my words, then you might leave the meeting angry, and, worse yet, you might even quit." I realized that he didn't want me to miss the vital point he felt I needed to hear, or potentially have me leave the meeting either upset or angry. "Mike, I want you to know that you are extremely important to me, not just as a valuable employee but also as a real friend." As was usual for Dick, he always started a difficult conversation with some positive remarks that built the person up.

As Dick began talking, I noticed that his hands were shaking a little and that he was extremely nervous. I could see his face tense up and even perspire a bit, like he would do at times, especially when he was anxious. Well, my mind was racing, as one would imagine, and I was desperately trying to figure out exactly what he wanted to talk to me about that made him so obviously nervous. I wondered if he felt I had done something wrong or possibly even improper, and I began to get a little nervous myself. I looked Dick right in the eye, hoping his gaze would comfort me. He went on to say, "Mike, in my opinion you are a highly competitive person, and often that is a real strength for you. I noticed over the years that you usually have to win at almost everything you do. Having said that, I think you have burned a few relationships because you are so competitive, and you need to learn how to back off at times and be willing to give and lose a battle here and there so that you could focus more on 'winning the war.' Mike, please don't take this the wrong way, but you need to develop more emotional empathy toward others, feel their feelings, so to speak, learn to care just a little more and not just make everything about the business decision."

I wasn't sure how to react at first, but I knew Dick cared about me and my family, and was doing his best as a leader and mentor to deliver some criticism with love and compassion.

That was one of the best lessons in leadership and humility I had ever witnessed from anyone other than my own father, certainly in the business world. I actually felt that Dick cared enough about me personally that he was willing to risk our relationship in order to help me grow as a person. It touched me deeply in so many ways.

I have never forgotten Dick's words, and throughout the years they have motivated me to grow and become the type of person and leader he knew I had the potential to someday achieve. Dick Freeman put my personal needs of growth and development in front of his own business—the one I was successfully running for him. He intuitively knew that if I took his mentorship advice the wrong way, that it could have easily caused me to leave the company. Dick's delicate balance between caring and counsel and the bottom line are hallmarks of his leadership style, lessons in life and work that I treasure to this very day.

CHAPTER 12

Money, Money, Money: Spending and Saving It Wisely

Never spend your money before you have earned it.
—Thomas Jefferson

Jack Welch, another one of the business leaders I most admire, said this: "I've learned that mistakes can often be as good a teacher as success." But, when those mistakes involve money, well, the fewer mistakes folks make the better!

No truer words may have ever been said when it comes to money. And not only do they apply to individuals but businesses and government, too. Our 2015 US federal national debt has skyrocketed to $18.2 trillion, and it is estimated that in 2016 it will be a whopping $19.334 trillion, according to federal government statistics. I would never run my business that way, or my household finances, and, in fact, by not practicing good financial literacy, including responsible debt management, Americans can never achieve what Dave Ramsey calls financial peace.

What is the definition of money? Money is an item of exchange commonly accepted by most people. It usually comes in the form of paper that a government created, and historically, those governments usually backed up their paper money with gold or silver. A few decades ago, the United States moved away from the gold standard and now backs up its paper money with the full faith and credit of the US government. Paper money only has a real value when the people accept it as such, and when the people lose faith in their government, then that paper quickly becomes relatively worthless. An example of this hyperinflation took place in Germany in the 1920s, when the exchange rate between the mark and the dollar was one trillion marks to one dollar. Before World War I, Germany was doing well, so this hyperinflation really took the German people by storm.

There were many reasons why Germany got to that point. The war was only supposed to last a short time, and the German government decided it was best to not have gold back up their currency anymore. They financed the war by borrowing money instead of using taxes or savings to pay the cost, therefore causing prices to skyrocket. To add to the problems, after Germany lost the war roughly four years later, it had to pay reparations of gold-backed marks under the Treaty of Versailles. The German economy was in shambles, and the high cost of living and rising prices forced the population to take their money out of their currency and put it into real goods such as real estate, diamonds, etc. The German government neglected to curb the inflation. In 1923, one US dollar equaled one trillion marks. That was Germany's breaking point.

But an amazing thing happened. With a new president came a new currency—the rentenmark. Even though it was still relatively worthless, nine zeros were struck from the currency, but the German people felt it had more value than it actually had in reality.

The reason I tell this story is to illustrate the importance of financial restraint and what can happen when money is manipulated and devalued. The same thing can happen to one's personal finances, which I know all too well.

Having made a ton of money in my thirties, I, too, learned some hard lessons about saving, keeping debt at bay, and taking personal financial responsibility.

My money came in the form of assets on my personal balance sheet such as real estate. After the Tax Reform Act of 1986, I saw firsthand what having too much debt relative to income could do. Even though on paper I was worth a fair amount, I was also heavily in debt, and that surely caused me undue financial pain and loss. I made up my mind then and there that working hard to earn a decent living and then spending my income wisely and prudently—and paying cash for most items—was a wiser path to follow.

Many people over the years have asked me what I mean by that personal mantra, and this is what I tell them. In our country, we have an almost intrinsic need to keep up with the Joneses. If the guy down the street has a bigger house, a newer car, or a cooler gadget, we have to do one better. Being bigger and better than the next guy trumps almost everything, even rational thought. I can't even begin to estimate how many folks' homes I've visited where the outside looks great, but the inside is empty. Why? Because they borrowed too much money to buy that house and, therefore, couldn't afford the furnishings. It was more important to be thought of as rich because of the size of their dwelling rather than wealthy in financial stability. I recall well the first house I personally bought and moved into back in 1979, located at 424 Ocala Court North in south Nashville. That house had three bedrooms and one and a half baths, and we only had enough furniture for one bedroom and the kitchen, plus a sofa and TV for the den. I was just like so many other young couples trying to do the best they could at the time.

The scriptures in 1Timothy 6:10 teach us that "the love of money is the root of all evil." Debt, in my opinion, is the root of all evil when it comes to financial freedom. People have asked me at times, "How can you advise individuals about not racking up debt when the US government owes money in the trillions of dollars?" That is the million-dollar question, for sure! In my opinion, too many folks just live for today and don't understand the difference between appreciating assets versus depreciating assets. Appreciating assets are those that have historically tended to go up in value over time such as a home, antiques, fine art, and other collectibles. They appreciate for many reasons, including the fluctuation of interest rates, or inflation, and an increase in demand or a weakening supply. A depreciating asset is one that typically goes down in value over time. A good example of this is a car. As soon as a person leaves the lot in his or her newly purchased automobile the car will go down in value, sometimes as much as 20 to 30 percent! The same goes for other items, such as televisions, household appliances, and even clothing. Using debt to finance someone's lifestyle is never a wise thing to do with the possible exception of financing a home. They are typically assets that appreciate in value over time and are also such large investments that it is very difficult to ever be able to save for them and pay cash.

Dave Ramsey has a great analogy that he calls the debt snowball. Basically, debt is like a snowball. First you start with a small amount of snow, and then you roll it back and forth until you gather more and more snow, and before you know it, the snowball is packed tightly with enough dense matter to make it snowball worthy. The same holds true for amassing debt. The more you accumulate, the more you spend paying back that debt in the form of interest, and then in a flash that debt snowballs uncontrollably, becoming unbearable and out of control; and the negative financial cycle continues.

So why, then, if this is so obvious, do people just abandon all reason and not think about their financial futures? It all boils down to the fact that we want too much, we want it immediately, and we borrow to the hilt to satisfy those impulses. That is the American dream gone rogue! And it all starts in childhood.

All any parent has to do is turn on a television, a computer, or iPad, and the evidence is overwhelming. Buy this new gadget, order this new toy, or call this number to get the one and only something. These advertising messages ingrain in our children that objects will make us happy, and we need to have them and have them immediately if we are to be looked upon as cool or successful. Add to that a culture in which many young people believe they are entitled to almost everything; well to me, that's a prescription for financial disaster. I truly believe that the only items we are entitled to in this life are our own opinions! Other than that, the true measure of success is hard work and leaving something behind for the people you love. Proverbs 13:22 teaches us that "a good person leaves an inheritance to their children's children."

While there are many different definitions of the word "success," I read one definition that rang true. It was: "Success is having enough to do what God has called you to do." At the end of life, that is really what will matter most—doing whatever it is that defines success in one's life.

That's why early in my own children's lives, I would often take a few minutes to talk with them about wants versus needs. For example, when they would ask me if they could buy a toy, I would say to them, "Do you really want this toy, or do you need it?" Obviously, they learned quickly and would tell me that the toy was a "want." I would then talk to them about where money comes from—namely hard work done persistently and consistently over time—and I would discuss with them how much money a person typically earns in one week. Once I went through that discussion, I would lead them to think through how long a person would have to work to earn enough money after he or she pays taxes to actually be able to purchase that toy. Usually they would see that it might take an entire week or more to earn enough money to buy the toy. I would continue the conversation by talking to them about how they would pay for their food or heat for their house if they spent all their money on a toy. As they got a little older, I taught them about interest and how using debt to purchase assets such as furniture or cars could destroy their ability to ever get ahead in life financially. Even though my children were young at the time, I explained the value of money. Over the years as they grew, they began to understand and appreciate these lessons. Now as adults they fully get it! It is never too early to teach children how to responsibly handle and value money, and it will save parents from having to deliver a tough-love lesson later.

Benjamin Franklin once said, "Money has never made man happy, nor will it, there is nothing in its nature to produce happiness. The more of it one has the more one wants." To illustrate that point empirically, a recent Harvard study measured groups of adults to see if there was a direct correlation between giving and receiving and happiness.

The study, which also involved Simon Fraser University and UBC, gave participants five dollars or twenty dollars, and they were asked to spend the money they received by the end of the day. One group was instructed to spend the money on themselves and the other group on someone else of their choice. The study participants were then divided in half, so each, regardless of having five or twenty dollars to spend, had a choice to spend even greater amounts on themselves or give that money to someone in need. What happened? When each group was asked what made them happier, spending the money on their own needs or knowing the money they gave away helped someone else, they unanimously said that they were happier giving to others. As the Bible in Acts 20:35 says, "It is more blessed to give than to receive."

Ronald Reagan echoed the same sentiment when he said, "We can't help everyone, but everyone can help someone."

The truth of the matter is that we Americans are far off track in amassing money to serve as a barometer of happiness. We want too many material things that we either don't need or simply can't afford. We live for the moment, borrow too much to get what we want, and fail to plan for the future, though we usually don't think of it that way. Wise people know that it takes much time and effort to accumulate anything of real and lasting value. They understand the value of "sowing" and "reaping." The Bible teaches us in Galatians 6:7 that "whatsoever a man soweth that shall he also reap." If we sow bad seeds, we will always reap a bad harvest. In financial terms, if we utilize our money making bad decisions based on keeping up with others, or just wanting too many things we really don't need, then we should not be surprised to grow well into our adult years and have hardly saved anything.

Sadly, that is where many Americans find themselves today. Their profile is an all too familiar one—poor spending and saving habits developed at a young age, the belief that money is the source of happiness, poor impulse control and the fallacy that accumulating debt is acceptable, and not having a strategic money plan for the future. When folks make poor financial decisions, they end up having to suffer from the natural consequences that always follow. President Theodore Roosevelt once said, "In any moment of decision, the best thing you can do is the right thing, the next best thing is the wrong thing, and the worst thing you can do is nothing."

So in the spirit of Roosevelt's wisdom, and my own personal and professional experience, I would offer some simple solutions to achieving financial security and managing money wisely and for the long term. I am convinced that anyone—regardless of how much money he or she makes—can plan for a solid financial future.

Like I was able to do after losing almost everything we had due to the repercussions of the Tax Reform Act of 1986, anyone can turn their financial situation around. What it definitely requires is an understanding of the difference between wants versus needs. It's not that complicated or even difficult to achieve. Dave Ramsey, in his book *Financial Peace*, points to what he calls the Seven Baby Steps. They are:

Baby step 1. $1,000 to start an emergency fund
Baby step 2.   Pay off all debt but the house
Baby step 3.   Accumulate three-to-six months of savings
Baby step 4.   Invest 15 percent of household income into retirement
Baby step 5.   Save for college fund for children
Baby step 6.   Pay off a home mortgage early
Baby step 7.   Build wealth and give

I like to equate them to the psychologist Abraham Maslow's well-regarded 1943 paper, *A Theory of Human Motivation*, in which he describes his theory of the "Hierarchy of Needs," which basically says that all human beings, before they can achieve the ultimate goal of self-actualization, must have their basic needs met, such as water, food, shelter, etc., before they can go on and become enlightened, so to speak. He used a pyramid to illustrate that concept with the basic human needs at the bottom—physiological and safety, and moving up the pyramid—love and belonging, esteem and self-actualization. The same goes for money, I believe. Folks need to take small steps to eliminate debt and learn to manage money before they can achieve that financial peace, or rise to the top of the pyramid.

I've created what I call Mike's Money Meter, to give folks some engaging ways to gauge their financial health and take those small but necessary steps to turn their finances into long-term mechanisms for growth and prosperity.

Here's how it works. On a scale of one to ten, with one being least likely and ten being most likely, rate yourself on each of the ten following money habits. If your score is between seventy-five and one hundred, then keep up the good work. If your score is between fifty and seventy-five, you need to focus on fixing those money habits with the lowest numbers, and if your score is below fifty, get some professional money management advice as soon as you can to secure your financial future.

1. You don't view money as the most important thing in life, and you live below your annual net income by spending less than you make.
2. You have established an emergency fund of at least $1,000.
3. You save 10 percent of your net income on a monthly basis.
4. You have paid off all debt except your home mortgage.
5. After having established a minimum savings account balance of six months of your normal living expenses, you invest 15 percent of your net income for retirement.
6. You have a checking account that you balance on a monthly basis.
7. You avoid the use of credit cards until your personal net worth exceeds $1 million, and you pay the full credit card balance each and every month to avoid the very high interest rates charged.
8. You have a college fund established and fund it monthly until the balance has grown to a minimum of $80,000 per child.
9. You make an extra monthly payment on your mortgage every year.
10. You consciously make an effort to help others by charitable giving with the goal of giving away a minimum of 10 percent of your net income annually.

Mike Hardwick

The bottom line is this: money can be a person's best friend or his or her worst enemy. It can provide a comfortable lifestyle, help others in need, and give folks the freedom to enjoy their lives in retirement. But it can also, if not managed properly, cause extreme pain and suffering. In my over forty years in the financial industry and from my own personal experience, I have seen what happens when folks spend like they are rich even though they are not, trying to keep up with their friends and neighbors. Earning money and spending it wisely are all too often diametrically opposed behaviors, though they should be practiced in tandem.

While practice does make perfect in many instances, I also know that we all make mistakes, and there is in reality no real perfect, especially when it comes to money. As I like to say, the goal is progress, not perfection! It's important to work hard at this mental discipline; don't be overly hard on yourself for the occasional misstep, and take the small steps to become a savvy financial consumer.

Another very well-known business hero of mine, Steve Jobs, talked about the role of money in his life. He said, "Bottom line is, I didn't return to Apple to make a fortune. I've been very lucky in my life and already had one. When I was twenty-five, my net worth was $100 million or so. I decided then that I wasn't going to let it ruin my life. There's no way you could ever spend it all, and I don't view wealth as something that validates my intelligence."

In terms of money, wiser words may never have been said!

CHAPTER 13

The Foundation of Giving Back: Why I Dedicate My Life to Service

> We make a living by what we get, but we make a life by what we give.—Winston Churchill

Being a person who gives back to others in their moment of need isn't exclusively a behavior of the rich and famous, as Bill Gates said. Americans have always been a generous group, reaching out to people who need help here in the United States and around the world, especially during times of great tragedy. We have seen this collective generosity in situations such as the aftermath of September 11; Hurricanes Katrina and Sandy; Japan's tsunami; the Haiti, Pakistan, and China earthquakes; the BP oil spill; and so many others. When a crisis occurs, the American people have selflessly reached into their wallets and hearts helping to lessen the trauma of victims directly affected by those unfathomable tragedies. Bill Gates once said, "The general idea of the rich helping the poor, I think, is important."

The National Philanthropic Trust reported that charitable giving is at an all-time high, with Americans giving a total of $358.38 billion in 2014, with the average household contributing $2,974 annually. Corporate giving was on the rise, too, with companies giving $17.77 billion to charity—a 13.7 percent increase from 2103. Foundations also reported increased giving in 2014, contributing $53.7 billion, an 8.2 percent increase from 2013. Recently I read that there are approximately one million charities in the United States that raise about $200 billion annually. This is encouraging news!

For people who do have means, though, I believe it is an obligation and one that many philanthropists take very seriously.

Billionaires such as Bill Gates, Warren Buffet, Barry Diller, Diane Von Furstenberg, Carl Icahn, David Rubenstein, and many others have signed what is now known as the Giving Pledge, where they have committed to give more than half of their wealth to charitable causes they support either during their lifetime or in their wills. The idea came about when Bill and Melinda Gates and Warren Buffet talked to many wealthy philanthropists around the world about the problems humanity faced, such as disease, poverty, hunger, homelessness, illiteracy, and terrorism, among many others, and ways in which they could collectively help. The participants were not asked to sign a contract to take this pledge. To the contrary, they have all agreed to give away their fortunes with a handshake and a moral commitment, promising to uphold the giving pledge as part of membership in this exclusive philanthropic club. Recently, another billionaire, Facebook founder Mark Zuckerberg, announced that he and his wife would give away 99 percent of Facebook's stock, worth billions and billions of dollars.

Growing up relatively poor, making a lot of money, and then almost losing it all, I know what it feels like to live with financial insecurity and worry about the basics such as how I was going to feed my family. While I always tried to help as many people as I could over the years, both personally and through my companies, I always knew at some point I would formalize the process and start a charitable foundation of my own.

But it all had to start somewhere. In looking back, I recall my parents always helping others even when they didn't have much money of their own. There were times when Dad and Mom would take folks out to lunch or dinner after church. Dad always paid for everyone, and then when we all got in the car afterward, Mom would say, "Honey, are you sure we have enough money to keep doing this?" I remember Dad trying to reassure Mom by saying, "Montelle, the Lord will take care of us if we do things with the right heart and motive, and, besides, helping others is always the right thing to do." Needless to say, those car rides set the stage for my own need to live up to their generous expectations, though at the time I didn't know it.

I also developed my love for giving and helping others from my mentor Dick Freeman. He was always giving gifts to others, especially my family and me. He was an exceptionally generous man. I watched him many times make purchases such as electronics or household appliances, where he would negotiate a much lower price and then literally buy all of the items the store had in stock. He would keep them stored in the attic of his house and over time dole them out to people he felt were in need.

I especially remember him leaving waiters and waitresses very large tips after a meal. He would say to me, "Mike, these folks work so hard. Can you imagine them being on their feet all day for such a little amount of money? By me leaving a one hundred dollar tip, well, that might just make the difference between that person being able to take care of his or her children or even buying enough food to feed them." It was not something that Dick did just during Christmas or other holidays either, but something he was happy to do all the time.

I recall taking Dick to lunch one day to a very nice restaurant on the west side of Nashville. As the waitress came over to us to take our order, he joked with her that I was the one responsible for the bill that day but that I was not known to be a very good tipper. He said to her, "Young lady, this man here isn't known for being a generous tipper, so here's twenty dollars for your time today." Dick handed her a twenty dollar bill. When she came back to our table to bring us our water and sweet tea, he told her again that he was really concerned about how little a tip I might leave her, so he gave her yet another twenty dollars. You could see how happy but surprised she was, and when she returned to our table with the food, Dick said, "Thank you, young lady. You are a very good waitress, and I don't want my friend here to leave without giving you the tip you deserve so here's another twenty dollars." By this time she was obviously shocked by Dick's generosity, and I estimated that when we had finished our meal, he had tipped the young lady about one hundred dollars! By this one small act of kindness, not only did the waitress feel good about herself and the job she was doing, but it made all three of us quite happy. This was vintage Dick Freeman! I just loved seeing the joy in Dick's eyes when he gave one of these gifts to someone; giving to others was clearly his true vocation.

These acts of random kindness made a real impression on me over the years. One day I decided to calculate how much money *I* could donate to a waiter or waitress myself, if *I* just left a one hundred dollar tip twice a week. That total over the course of a year came out to about $10,000. Frankly, that was really nothing to me in the context of how much income I was blessed to make annually at that time, and yet, I knew how much it meant to those folks who were working so hard just to get by. After doing the math, I made a decision to never worry again about trying to figure out what a 15 or 20 percent tip was, but rather to just be overly generous. I knew how blessed I was having such wonderful and giving parents who taught me well the lesson from 2 Corinthians 9:7 in the Bible, which tells us that "the Lord loves a cheerful giver." Further, that part of scripture also says, "He who sows sparingly will also reap sparingly, and he who sows bountifully will also reap bountifully." With those words in mind, having Dick Freeman as a mentor in my life was yet another tangible and wonderful blessing. The lessons I learned from these experiences were priceless life lessons in my book.

During the earlier years when I was not making the kind of annual income that I later was blessed to make, I would do as Dad and Mom did, namely help feed the hungry and do volunteer work for charities and, of course, our church. As Abraham Lincoln said, "To ease another's heartache is to forget one's own." While I did not at that time in my life have much monetarily, I was more than able to volunteer my time to help others.

My parents also taught me through the scriptures: "It is more blessed to give than to receive" (Acts 20:35); "To whom much is given, much is expected" (Luke 12:48); and "You cannot out give God" (Luke 6:38). I would define philanthropy in those terms, as one who has much and is willing or motivated to give out of his or her abundance to others in real need. Sadly, over the years I have seen people give their time and hard-earned money to people or charitable organizations that did not really have a true need, or would spend their donation dollars on excessive overheads and salaries. So I always tried to really determine if the person or persons I am working to help are folks that truly are down on their luck. For example, I rarely will stop to give to someone some money who is begging on the side of the road holding a sign asking for help. Rather, I want to get to know the person and what is happening in his or her life before I give the person a donation; I want to ascertain their real need. In a December 25, 2015, *USA Today* article, Princeton University Professor Peter Singer was quoted as saying, "Simply giving to get a warm glow, giving to the person on the street who holds out a cup or giving to a charity that shows you a brochure of a smiling child, that may or may not be doing good."

The Bible teaches us that there is no problem finding folks who really need help. Deuteronomy 15:11 says, "There will always be poor people." My goal is to make sure that I do as much to help others as I can and know that the folks I am blessed to help are those who truly have the greatest need. Fortunately, there are organizations such as Charity Navigator where people can go and see just how charities are spending their money, so anyone who makes a donation can do it with accurate information.

One example of my early strategic philanthropy strategy is the story about a woman in our church who was struggling financially and also personally. Many years ago, someone told me about this single lady who would attend services every week but always looked so sad and despondent. She was also a mother with a little girl in elementary school at the time.

She would rarely smile, and I came to learn that was because she was self-conscious about her smile and desperately needed teeth.

Apparently, she had lost most of her teeth because she was very poor and was never financially able to go to the dentist, and was uneducated about the importance of good dental hygiene. As a result, she had never practiced good eating habits, probably eating poor quality foods, or drinking soda with way too much sugar, for example, and her few remaining teeth were in very, very bad shape. She was experiencing a lot of pain as well, and for anyone who has ever had tooth or gum pain, it can be excruciating, to say the least. I decided the best way to help her was to contact a good friend of mine who was a dentist in town. I asked him to reach out to this lady and help her get a new set of dentures. The only prerequisite was that I would pay the bill, but he was not to reveal who was taking care of the expense.

My heart just went out to this lady and her little girl every single time I saw them at church, so I would always make it a habit to talk to them. After getting her a new set of teeth and watching her regain confidence and carry herself with dignity and pride, I so wanted to help her and her child even more. I decided that I would be more of an encourager each time I ran into them. I would ask the little girl, "How do you like school, and how are your grades?" I could see that she was happy for the attention, and so at one point I asked the little girl to bring me a copy of her next report card, and for every A she received, I would give her ten dollars. Well, that seemed to really motivate her, and about four weeks later, she came running up to me in church one Sunday, hardly able to contain her enthusiasm. "Mr. Mike, look, I made two As on my report card!"

"That is wonderful, honey; I'm so proud of you. Here is the $20 for those two As, and I hope you keep up the good work." She smiled, took the money, and left church with her mom feeling good about her accomplishment. Believe it or not, I continued my offer of ten dollars for every A on her report card throughout her years in elementary school, middle school, and high school. I was so proud of her, and was delighted to give her the money. She eventually went to college, earned her degree in education, and today is a school teacher in Nashville.

I have found among the greatest and purest joys in life is giving and helping others. I am convinced that it really is more blessed to give than to receive!

As a result of this tenet, and my personal experiences with philanthropy, I decided to formalize a giving process not just for myself, but for my company. That was the genesis of what is now called, the Churchill Foundation.

Bill Gates said about the importance of philanthropy, "Effective philanthropy requires a lot of time and creativity—the same kind of focus and skills that building a business requires."

Taking Bill Gates's advice, I put the kind of time and energy I put into building Churchill Mortgage into a structure for our new foundation. I began thinking about it in earnest probably about four or five years ago. I noticed a few of my friends, such as Dave Ramsey and Lee Beaman, had done the same thing, so I began talking with several different friends individually about how they put their own foundation together and the steps they took to get it operational. I wanted it to not only reflect the core values of our company but also have our employees feel part of the process, which is always how I've managed Churchill Mortgage.

According to the National Center for Charitable Statistics, more than one million nonprofit organizations are registered in the United States. In that group are also private foundations, just like ours. In fact, the Internal Revenue Service estimates that there are more than 115,000 private foundations in the country, which just reinforces my belief that Americans are among the most caring and giving people on earth. Some of those private foundations are large, while others are medium or small; still, each plays a role in improving the quality of life for people who are less fortunate or who are in need following a disaster of any kind.

As the *Saturday Night Live* actor and comedian Darell Hammond said about how he was helped as a child by the kindness of others: "I was raised in a group home for fourteen years, so I was a beneficiary of philanthropy. I didn't have a family. The nameless, faceless strangers were my family. They gave me an education, put food on the table and clothes on my back. I am who I am because of that formative experience. Now I am paying it forward."

Many of our employees have volunteered in nonprofits, some for homeless shelters and the group homes where Darell Hammond and Jimmy Wayne grew up. That's why it was so important for me when I was thinking about how to structure our foundation to really engage our employees, and I liked the idea of using this as yet another way of having my four children even more involved in helping others and developing their own philanthropic styles. I knew that over time I would be able to fully fund the foundation and that the board, comprised of my kids, Matt Clarke, and Cecil Kemp, would really help put more thought and structure to it. We also have an employee advisory board of twelve folks who are excited to be part of the process. (To date, I have put about $700,000 in the account, and our goal is to increase that amount up to at least $5 million over the next five years, and then grow it from there.)

The group is also working on not just the structure of the Churchill Foundation, but also on giving guidelines and a process for receiving applications and handing out grants. As I've said, having a strategic approach to giving is very important to me, and identifying areas where we want to be involved is critical for success. We know that education, homelessness, veterans, and hunger are issues we want to target, and over time we will uncover even more areas of giving that will help those in need in the Churchill Mortgage locations where we do business. Cecil Kemp, who by the way is the author of well over twenty books on mentorship and leadership, and has consulted with thousands of CEOs over his stellar career, has been very instrumental in using his considerable management experience in helping the foundation codify its giving strategy.

"Churchill Mortgage is what I would call a 'relationship-centered organization, not a transactional focused one' and by that I mean they try to hire only those people with kind hearts, because they know that anyone can be trained to understand the mortgage business, but no one can be trained to be kind, thoughtful and empathetic; either it's in them or not," Cecil has said to us many times. I am grateful that this wonderful man and a friend of mine for more than thirty years, has also worked with me and our management team on areas such as emotional intelligence, which has been proven to be more of a factor in business success than any other skill set. Emotional intelligence or EQ refers to someone's ability to identify, utilize, understand, and manage emotions and use the skill to resolve problems in the workplace as well as defeat challenges and obstacles in life generally. Many scientific studies by psychologists, leadership experts such as Cecil, and other management gurus have quantified the impact of EQ in the business environment; I have seen this firsthand throughout my career.

Cecil also has helped give the foundation an overarching focus on specific areas on which we want to concentrate. Jesus preached that those who are most in need are "widows, orphans and prisoners." Well, not literally just folks in jail, in our case, but those who are imprisoned by addiction, mental illness, or any other situation that has hijacked their souls, so to speak. He's also led the board's thinking that we would rather not give out many small donations but instead give larger financial grants to fewer organizations, allowing us to make an even larger impact on the communities we serve.

Another one of our Churchill family members who is instrumental in the foundation is our vice president of marketing, Marisa Shapter, who has been with Churchill for the past eleven years. She came to us from AT&T wireless with a degree in finance and rose up the ranks from an entry-level position to now an officer of the company. She has embraced our culture of giving and works very hard to hire people who share the same values and who she identifies as having a generous heart and spirit. She is putting that same energy into the foundation's guidelines and structure and all of the details that can make or break a charitable entity. I was very touched to watch her over the years become a philanthropist in her own right, giving of her time to help people from all walks of life both inside and outside of Churchill Mortgage.

An example of this was when we had a new employee who unexpectedly got sick and was taken to the hospital with a very serious condition that he did not know he had when we hired him. He also had a very pregnant wife at home who was expecting twins, and he was clearly worried about what would happen to them if he couldn't work. Marisa and many of our other employees came up with a plan that included giving the family money, preparing meals and taking them to his wife on a daily basis, and doing whatever they could to help this young family get through such a difficult time. I'm happy to report he recovered from his illness and is now one of our top producers!

If there is anything that I have learned over my career, it is empowering others to do great things. I know that my love for doing work that helps others has also filtered down to our four-hundred-plus employees; that couldn't make me more proud! I am reminded of a quote by John Andrew Holmes that illustrates this very well: "There is no better exercise for the heart than reaching down and lifting people up."

Over the years, they have done so much for others, and that spirit of giving has become part of Churchill's corporate culture. For example, our employees have cooked Thanksgiving meals and delivered them to veterans in transitional housing; visited veterans in VA hospitals; sorted food at food banks; raised money for breast cancer, the kidney foundation, and many others; and brought Christmas baskets to Nashville's homeless population, among so much more. As we at Churchill are fond of saying, "Giving is not just about making a donation; it's about making a difference!"

But sometimes financial donations can change lives, too, and so in 2105, the Churchill Foundation board agreed to match up to $24,000 in employee contributions. That means that if everyone in our Nashville office alone donated less than ten dollars from their paychecks, then the foundation would have $50,000 each year to give to deserving charities.

Because our employees are actively involved with the charitable giving process, and one of our foundation goals is to contribute funds to qualified nonprofits in which they are involved, we not only are able to know where the funds are going but also measure the success of the contribution.

In addition, we try being nimble in terms of meeting immediate needs of a qualified nonprofit organization or even an individual with a unique need that comes to our attention. For example, a few months ago I heard about a young wounded warrior, Army Specialist Tyler Jeffries, who lost both of his legs and suffered severe injuries when he stepped on an improvised explosive device (IED) while on patrol in Afghanistan. In fact, I remembered hearing his name on Fox News when he was visiting President Bush—both forty-one and forty-three—and first ladies Barbara and Laura at their home in Kennebunkport, Maine, and proposed to his girlfriend, Lauren, right in front of them. Apparently, he was short on funds for his wedding. The Churchill Foundation was able to cut him a check for $2,500, and within a week we had it mailed to his home just outside Charlotte, North Carolina. I'm told we will be invited to their wedding, and look forward to being part of this wonderful moment in their young lives.

No matter if a person gives $1 million, $1 billion, or $10, every little bit helps. And if they also volunteer their time—no matter what the cause, or simply reach out to someone who they believe needs their help—that can make all the difference. I am humbled to witness the generosity and compassion of my family both at home and in the workplace. It is not a cliché to say that one believes in paying it forward. Every person on God's great earth has the ability to change someone else's life if he or she would simply open his or her eyes and see the need.

An example of this is the iconic story about the boy and the starfish that has been widely quoted, and yet, no one really knows who wrote the tale. It goes something like this. A man was walking along a deserted beach at sunset. As he walked, he could see a young boy in the distance. As he drew nearer, he noticed that the boy kept bending down, picking something up, and throwing it into the water. Time and again he kept hurling things into the ocean. As the man approached even closer, he was able to see that the boy was picking up starfish that had been washed up on the beach, and one at a time he was throwing them back into the ocean. The man asked the boy what he was doing, and the boy replied, "I am throwing these washed up starfish back into the ocean, or else they will die through lack of oxygen,"

"But," the man said, "You can't possibly save them all; there are thousands on this beach, and this must be happening on hundreds of beaches along the coast. You can't possibly make a difference."

The boy looked down and was frowning for a moment; then he bent down to pick up another starfish, smiling as he threw it back into the sea. He replied, "I made a huge difference to that one!"

I would equate our foundation to the foundation of a house. If it is built with a solid footing, poured with patience and persistence, and designed to last for many years, then it will provide a lifetime of physical and emotional shelter. We should do nothing less for those who are the much-deserved recipients of our foundation's financial support.

CHAPTER 14

The Power of Progress, Not Perfection

Our greatest glory is not in never failing, but in rising up every time we fail.—Ralph Waldo Emerson

I spent the first half of my life chasing a great career and some level of perfection; the second half not so much. Like NFL quarterback Tim Tebow once said about his own career ups and downs: "I'm not perfect. And who knows how many times I've fallen short. That's the amazing thing about the grace of God."

It took that life-changing conversation with my buddy Mike Ballard to turn my life around. When I was at my lowest point emotionally, spiritually, and financially, Ballard with one simple sentence, "Mike, you know what your problem is? You lost your faith in God," unwittingly gave me the tools to realize this: that no human being is perfect, and I am no exception.

There is an interesting article I read in *Psychology Today* by Dr. Adrian Furnham called "The Curse of Perfectionism." He examines the positive and negative qualities of being that type of person who can never make a mistake, is held to often unrealistic high standards, and where failure is not an option. Many of those high standards are self-imposed, while others are reinforced in occupations, such as professional sports, where ultraperformance matters. But, as Dr. Furnham reveals, there is also a dark side. "Perfectionism is seen as a cause and correlate of serious psychopathology. At worst, perfectionists believe they should be perfect—no hesitations, deviations, or inconsistencies. They are super-sensitive to imperfection, failing and weakness. They believe their acceptance and lovability is a function of never making mistakes. And they don't know the meaning of 'good enough.' For them, it's always all or nothing."

I can relate to the good doctor's words only too well. As a recovering perfectionist, I realized that when I sought perfection, I was always disappointed. I could never get there. I always fell short! Perfection is simply not possible, but here's what I can seek each and every day—progress! That I can realize if I only try. In fact, that has become my own personal mantra over the years, namely, progress, not perfection.

But achieving progress, not perfection, did not come easily to me. It was a slow and steady evolution of my learning how to have faith in God, listening instead of giving orders, focusing on family and friendships, and developing an emotional intelligence, to name just a few. And there was one pivotal moment that also helped to change my perfectionist personality, and, of all things, it happened over dinner at my parents' house.

I can remember it as if it was yesterday, though it was probably more than twenty years ago. Dad had called me and invited me to dinner and was planning to grill some steaks and the usual fixings to go with it. As usual, I had a few employee issues come up, so I didn't leave the office until well after 6:30 PM, an hour late for dinner. I finally pulled up to their driveway, and Dad was out in the backyard already grilling the steaks. As I walked out on the back patio, I apologized for being late, and Dad responded in his usual kind and concerned way by saying, "Son, sit down and relax. What made you so late anyway?"

"Dad, it was an issue that came up with a couple of my employees, and I had to stay a little longer at the office to take care of it." I went on to tell him some of those issues. Just as I was finishing my sentence, Dad gave me *that* look, the facial expression I have seen on his face over my entire life. It was a combination of pure concern with a tiny bit of annoyance thrown in to achieve maximum impact. After all, Dad was a pastor and the master of communicating to achieve a desired result. Right away I knew he was about to say something that would have some sort of silent yet implied lesson that he wanted to make sure I understood.

"My goodness, son," Dad said, "I guess I didn't realize how little you cared about your employees."

I was stunned. "Dad, what are you talking about? Of course I care about them; that's why I was late." He calmly continued to turn the steaks over on the grill, sprinkling them with a little salt and pepper while I again tried to explain more precisely what I felt was an issue with some of my employees, who were not being focused enough and taking care of business. After a few minutes of me going on and on, Dad, ever the consummate pastor, went on to explain what he meant by my not caring.

"Mike, this is what I mean," Dad said. "You were late for dinner because work came first. You were setting such a high standard for yourself that being on time wasn't your first priority. Mom and I and your wife and children came second. Now, your employees see you working late, trying to be perfect all the time, and don't you realize they want to be just like you? That is asking way too much of them. They can't be perfect all the time. Maybe they are having a bad day, maybe they don't feel well, or they are having trouble at home."

He then went on to ask me a simple question. "Son, how many years have I been pastoring our church?"

"Well, I think it must be in the forty-year range," I responded, still wondering where he was going with that question.

"Mike, for those forty or so years can you estimate just how many sermons and lessons I had to prepare for over all those years?"

"Well," I said, "assuming you preached about forty-five Sunday mornings and another forty-five Sunday evenings every year, and another forty-five Sunday school lessons after that, plus forty-five Wednesday evening Bible studies you taught each year, not to mention those revivals you preached at various churches, I would say you have probably had to prepare at least seven thousand to eight thousand sermons and lessons over your pastoring career."

"Wow, son, that's a lot of sermons and lessons. Do you think that over these past forty years or so that I was always on my A game each and every time?"

"Well, Dad," I said, "I never thought about that. But I know you always took your job very seriously."

Dad looked at me with his quintessential kind expression and said, "Son, you were with me most of those years growing up in our house, right? I'm sure you recall a few times in the car on the way to church when your mother and I probably had some disagreements. Do you really think that I was able to just quickly turn that off and preach my best sermons on those Sunday mornings? Don't you think I might not have been feeling well sometimes? And what about those times when I was a little under the weather or just had other things troubling me?"

"Dad, I really never thought about it that way," I said. "I am sure you had times when you just weren't at your very best."

"Mike, during all those years of working did you ever take a Friday off, play golf, or just not get enough sleep? Did you ever go to work with a bad cold or even the flu? Your employees are human, too, and nobody—not you or I—could give 100 percent all of the time. I am not saying you should ever accept mediocrity from an employee, or even allow someone to take advantage of your good graces, but if you can get folks to give you a solid 75 to 80 percent, that's pretty good. You should appreciate that, be good, and take care of them if you really care about them. They will be much more inclined to give their best for you when they know how much you really do care."

Then it hit me! "Man, Dad, you're so right! How can I expect 100 percent effort and focus from my own employees when I'm not always on my A game myself?" I replied. By that point in the conversation, I knew exactly what he meant. He ended with this point, "Son, folks don't care how much you know until they know how much you care!"

That was an impactful lesson for me and helped me begin to change my thinking about why we, as a nation, expect so much from our employees and ourselves. After all, we may be the only country in the world that doesn't have laws setting the amount of hours in a workweek—134 others do. I believe this unrealistic work ethic has its roots in a number of factors, including the overvalue of money, the collapse of the family unit in our country, which is causing higher and higher rates of divorce, the need to keep up with others, and other cultural values that have been drilled into workers' heads for generations. This overemphasis on perfection has no better champion than in the world of sports.

Since I am a sports fan, I have seen over the years the toll that perfection has taken on athletes, for whom way too much has been expected. Rather than allowing them to make small gains over time, many coaches have expected nothing less than perfection from them during each and every game. But, as I tell my employees, making mistakes is part of life, and as long as they do their best, I have no expectations of them being perfect.

I can illustrate my theory that progress not perfection will make folks happier and more productive with this example of Butch Jones, head football coach of the University of Tennessee (UT). When UT hired Coach Jones back in 2012, the football program had fallen on some hard times. While being the eighth winningest football program in college history, UT had been in a grueling five-to-six-year drought, one that rabid fans like me found hugely disappointing.

Coach Jones recognized, skillfully, that in order to turn things around he had to change the perfectionist culture that had been allowed to seep into the UT athletic program over many years. He started by talking about how important it was to take care of the little things first. Those little things included respecting and valuing people, not just the players, but also all the other employees in the UT athletic department, from the ball boys and laundry guys to the cafeteria folks who helped make sure the players ate a well-balanced diet. He then came up with a theme each year for the program, with the first year theme being brick by brick, and the second year's theme 1 percent. His goal with each theme was to help every single person in the athletic program understand the high value in making solid progress in every area every day. He wisely knew that achieving small but important goals would make his players and, in fact, the entire UT family, recognize their success, and not be afraid of failure.

Well, I'm happy to report that over the past couple of years, UT is back to slowly winning and regaining its national prominence, thanks to Coach Jones. The team has gone to back to back bowl games, and fills Neyland Stadium each Saturday with well over one hundred thousand enthusiastic UT football fans! The belief is back, and as he continues to make progress, the winning culture is gaining tremendous momentum and support, not just from the players, but also from each and every person in the athletic department, across the university, and from the hundreds of thousands of UT fans. Coach Jones is a great example of someone who embraces the axiom that progress, not perfection, is one of the primary keys to a happy and healthy work and personal life.

Though not a sports icon, I think most everyone would agree that Nelson Mandela, the South African leader who was imprisoned for twenty-seven years in an eight-by-eight cell, was a man of uncompromising strength and dignity. Not only did he fight against apartheid, a terrible system of white minority rule, but he united his country and led it to democracy and freedom for all its citizens. But what strikes me the most about Mandela was how he embraced his flaws—his troubled youth, relationship issues, and others. He once said, "One of the most difficult things is not to change society but to change yourself." He truly believed that good things will happen if you stay the course and don't expect perfection.

Over the years I have tried to instill that philosophy in all of my employees, and I'm very proud to say that for the most part it is working.

In the financial services industry, like professional sports, being the best is always expected, and there is no room for anything less. In the 1987 Oliver Stone film *Wall Street*, Michael Douglas played the ruthless corporate raider Gordon Gekko, a man obsessed by greed and the pursuit of perfection. His quest for greed over good led him to his eventual demise, using inside information provided by one of his employees as a way to make big money on illegal trades. Eventually, the Securities and Exchange Commission got wind of his insider trading. To make matters worse, his former employee used a wire device to record Gekko giving the details of his crime. While the film was a pretty dramatic example of greed gone wild and the quest for being on top and being perfect, still, many hard-charging Wall Street types know exactly what it means to have no room for error.

In our Churchill Mortgage culture, we reinforce to our employees each and every day that while we know they may not always be on their A game, like Dad said to me during that life-changing moment at his house, that is okay by me. It warms my heart to know that our employees realize that in order to become the best they can be, they need to keep chopping wood and realize that progress not perfection is the ultimate goal. As a result they can relax, take a breath, and focus on their long-term success despite the pitfalls along the way.

An example of this thinking, and in our case, corporate philosophy, is another story about one of our newer employees, who thought she had made the mistake of a lifetime and was going to pay dearly for that. She had been on the phone with a potential client, going over the terms of the mortgage application, and explaining to the client just how much their mortgage would cost if they put down a standard twenty percent of the price of the home and how the interest rate would vary depending upon the terms they decided to choose. She was very excited to be closing one of her first loans and forgot that she needed to have her supervisor approve the transaction before she finalized it with the customer. The way the story was told to me was that her supervisor reviewed her work and recognized immediately that she had not calculated the numbers accurately, and, as a result, it would cost us well over an additional $5,000.

She was mortified. So much so that she started to cry and told her supervisor that she would resign from the company because of making such a serious mistake. Instead, her supervisor took her by the hand, led her to her office and said this: "Listen, we all make mistakes, Beth. I know you are upset because you think you have really failed and cost us a lot of money. Yes, you did cost us about $5,000, and I hope that won't happen in the future, but let's talk through what you did wrong and figure out how you can avoid making the same mistake in the future."

We had another situation where an employee of ours came to us from a big bank in the city and thought that his experience was superior to some of his peers, and he sure acted like that, too. It was obvious to other people as well. At some point I learned about it and wanted to chat with this young man myself. He was surely very talented and had a great future with us, but he clearly needed to know that in our business being the perfect know-it-all would just not fit in with our culture.

I sat him down one day and told him this: "I really respect your experience and you wanting to do well and let others know that on your team. The thing is that here at Churchill we are a family and a place where we look out for each other and never put our needs over someone else's. When I was your age, I thought I knew it all too, but I eventually learned the hard way that was not the case. I made so many very costly mistakes, many that I could have probably avoided had I been willing to listen to more experienced folks rather than thinking I was so smart. Thankfully, I was fortunate to have a couple of great mentors who invested in me and helped me learn so much through the years. So I'm giving you the benefit of my experience and hoping you will keep your mind open and try to learn as much as you can while you are here. Also, I would urge you to consider Proverbs 15:22, which teaches us that 'in the multitude of counselors there is safety.' If you seek solid counsel from several folks who you know have your best interests at heart and have wisdom from their own personal experiences, then I am sure you will experience much success and be here for many, many more years to come."

Sure enough, that young man followed my advice and has been one of our finest employees and someone others always look to for advice.

Ultimately, like the psychologist David Burns said in another article written in a 1980 *Psychology Today* issue, "Reaching for the stars, perfectionists may end up clutching at air." How true those words are even today. Often we equate being perfect with success and anything less than that means failure. These unrealistic standards—whether they be placed on professional athletes, CEOs, or any human being needs to change, otherwise we will be creating very unhappy and dissatisfied individuals. At the root is the desire to be socially acceptable to others, and I contend that we need to only be acceptable to God.

The bottom line is this: a person's worth is not measured by his or her latest and greatest accomplishment. He or she is not a success one moment and a failure another, rather a compilation of experiences—good and bad—that make the person a whole human being. Take it from me—a recovering perfectionist myself—that progress not perfection is the prescription for a life of fulfillment, happiness, and peace.

Chapter 15

The Business of Life: My Lessons Learned from Family, Faith, and the Bottom Line

A merry heart does good, like medicine.—Proverbs 17:22

Over the years many folks have asked me to write a book about my life. Frankly, I wasn't sure that anything I would have to say would be worth reading. Then something happened that changed the course of my thinking, but more about that later.

I believe that no matter what a person's net worth is, his or her position, power, or social standing, everyone is truly a child of God. The world works generally because it takes all of us to keep its parts moving. No roads, bridges, or buildings would be built without engineers or construction workers; no diseases treated or cured without physicians, researchers, or health-care workers; no food grown without farmers; and the list goes on infinitum. I guess in some sense one could agree with former Secretary of State Hillary Clinton when she said, "It takes a village!" But, no matter what a person does to contribute to the planet and its inhabitants, to me, there is one overarching quality that I truly believe is the key to happiness and fulfillment. Perhaps Luke 6:38 GNB says it best: "Give to others, and God will give to you. Indeed, you will receive a full measure, a generous helping, poured into your hands—all that you can hold. The measure you use for others is the one that God will use for you." Fortunately for me, I have seen firsthand the power of those words from the people who I admire most—my father and my mentor, Dick Freeman.

Lessons Learned from Family

Who would have guessed that Krispy Kreme doughnuts would have altered the course of my life in such a powerful and dramatic way? Dozens upon dozens of those sweet chocolate and glazed delicacies gave me the confidence to sell almost anything, and I owe it all to my parents!

As a young boy, I never could have imagined how those early Saturday mornings selling Krispy Kreme doughnuts and plate lunches in our Woodbine community to raise money for our church would have had such a profound impact on me. In those early hours, when all I wanted to do was stay in bed well after the sun came up, Dad gently prodded Steve and I to get moving and get ready for what I realize today was a major life lesson. That is, the value of hard work, to never give up or take no for an answer, and to positively impact the lives of others. The great Jamaican reggae singer, songwriter, and musician Bob Marley so eloquently said, "The greatness of a man is not in how much wealth he acquires, but in his integrity and his ability to affect those around him positively."

I've been more than blessed to have parents who were extremely loving, caring, and giving people. They not only gave so much of their time to help people in need, but they also used their personal financial resources for supporting many charitable causes within and outside of the church. Giving was their vocation and, more importantly, their passion!

Mom and Dad never failed to tithe, meaning giving 10 percent of their income to the church. The tithing system described in the Bible was designed specifically to meet the needs of the religious, economic, and political system of ancient Israel. Each of the twelve tribes of Israel, except the tribe of Levi, initially received an allotment of land in the promised land of Canaan. The Levites were supported by a tithe offering from the other eleven tribes. All the families of those eleven tribes were giving a tenth of all produce, flocks, and cattle to the Levites. In turn, the Levites were to give a tenth of that to support the priests. (Deuteronomy 26:12–13.) Tithes were also used to meet the needs of foreigners, orphans, and widows. (Deuteronomy 26:12–13.) In addition, everyone was to be generous to those in need.

Additionally, my parents were known all around Nashville for lending a helping hand in very personal ways too, such as handing out food to the hungry, helping folks make their rent payments so they would not be evicted from their homes, and even paying their utility bills so their heat would not be turned off in the dead of winter. And yet, my parents were never rich in the monetary sense. To the contrary, they rarely had any money left over by the end of most months to take care of their own personal expenses. God never provided financial rewards to them anywhere near what I have been so blessed to receive. Yet my parents were beyond blessed with literally thousands of wonderful friends that would do almost anything to help them in good times and bad. And, boy, did they ever!

It would be almost as easy to say the very same thing about my grandparents. They were all givers! As the French philosopher Albert Camus once said: "Blessed are the hearts that can bend; they shall never be broken." My parents' and grandparents' hearts were as vast at the Smokey Mountains and as flexible as a rubber band. They truly loved and cared for others. I strongly believe that God always provided for their every need, and many times even some of their "wants." Most of all, the lifelong friends that God provided them were grateful for their friendship, fellowship, and, maybe most importantly, their devoted trust and respect. In a very real and meaningful way, the chapter in Luke reflected so well my parents' lifelong philosophy: "As they gave to others, God gave to them!"

The life lessons I learned, not just from hearing my parents' words of wisdom, but also from watching them live their daily lives were invaluable. I must have heard Romans 13:7 quoted by my father a thousand times, which teaches us to, "give honor to whom honor is due." This scripture, together with so many more, helped teach me to believe in others, love and care for others, be kind and giving to others, and respect others. I am thankful every day of my life for parents and grandparents who knew the value and the power of those words and lived their lives accordingly.

Lessons Learned from Faith

It took me many years to *understand and internalize the true meaning of "faith."* And it took a good friend—Mike Ballard—to change my life with these few but powerful words, "Hardwick, you know what's wrong with you? You've lost your faith in God."

Too often life throws you curveballs. In my case, when the real estate market tanked following the Tax Reform Act of 1986, that ball hit me with the velocity of a Roger Clemens fastball! I was debilitated, not sure how or what to do to relieve my emotional and financial pain. Even though I grew up as the son of a preacher, studied theology, and went to church almost every Sunday of my life, still I was emotionally lost. I had not only lost most of my financial wealth, but worse, my faith in God wavered.

It is too easy at times to begin to doubt God, even when I was reared so deeply in the faith. When I was a child attending church as frequently as playing with my friends in the playground, it was easy to forget or not appreciate the need to have a truly strong belief or faith yourself. That might sound like it is a contradiction, but this unfettered devotion can instill a sense of transferred faith. By that I mean a person may have not personally experienced a strong belief and connection with God because he or she has only read scripture and not fully studied scripture. As a result, the person never established his or her own direct connection with God through the power of personal study and prayer. When that is the case, folks can easily stumble when life's inevitable curveballs are hurled toward them. When hard times come, as they always do, it becomes much easier to doubt and even question the faith that, heretofore, has always been one of life's constants.

In my experience, having a friend like Mike Ballard to confide in during those times when I doubted myself was a true blessing. Mike was not just a friend who cared about me and was there in my darkest hour, but a beacon of light when I needed it the most.

Mike Ballard was the antithesis of the friends of Job. The story of Job in the Old Testament tells the tale of a strongly devout man who loved God and was completely committed to God's purpose in his life. In many ways, Job was an illustrative example of a person of great virtue; yet, when his life took a turn for the worse, experiencing deep trials in his personal health and family, as well as massive financial losses, his friends literally abandoned him. He felt alone and experienced deep emotional issues of doubt, despair, discouragement, and confusion, and at times even questioned if God even cared about him at all! But, Job was blessed to have through his entire life a very personal and deep faith. Those qualities of belief and faith in an almighty God, who really loved and cared for him, eventually gave Job the strength to overcome his incredible trials, despite his supposed close friends mocking and ridiculing him.

Thankfully, Mike Ballard was not a friend like Job's friends! Instead, Mike was someone who was willing to be honest with me, confront me with what I needed to hear, and speak the truth to me at a time when I was wondering where God was and why he wasn't there for me. When I think about Mike, I often remember the phrase from the singer and actress Dionne Warwick's beautiful 1985 ballad, "That's What Friends Are For!" It took my friend, Mike Ballard to care enough about me to ask me the tough question I really needed to hear. This was a seminal moment in my life, and to this day, because of him, I have never wavered in my faith in the power and love of God.

Lessons Learned from the Bottom Line

I have learned so much about business from many different coaches, advisers, and the countless professional journals, business books, and magazine articles I have read and studied over my forty-plus years working for other people and owning my own businesses. Without having *ongoing mentors* in my life, I doubt I would have had the opportunity to test my limits, have the confidence to take risks, and look at failure as an opportunity to make things right. No matter what level a person is in business—from an entry-level worker to a CEO—the need to have guidance and support is a crucial element in giving people the confidence and purpose to achieve their dreams.

From my two mentors—my father and Dick Freeman—as well as other very influential people in my life such as, J. C. Bradford, Gordon Inman, Cecil Kemp, Dave Ramsey, Todd Duncan, and John Maxwell, I have learned the value of a number of leadership principles that are tried and true, not just theoretical. These leadership principles work, because they work. And, as someone who has tried to pass these words of wisdom along to my own employees and others in the mortgage banking industry, it is my sincerest hope that those who incorporate them into their own lives will benefit by them as much as I have. While it does take persistence to be able to do that, as I've often said, it's important to know that *progress, not perfection*, can go a long way toward helping someone realize his or her potential. Tom Black sent me a wonderful quote that illustrates this point so well. It was by the actor and director Cecil B. DeMille. He said, "Most of us serve our ideals by fits and starts. The person who makes a success of living is the one who sees his goal steadily and aims for it unswervingly. That is dedication."

And I would be remiss not to mention some of the lessons I have learned from the great Winston Churchill, my company's namesake. I chose him to be the steward of Churchill Mortgage because of what I have learned from him over the years and how he has influenced me to be an effective leader and problem solver. Churchill believed that there was no substitute for hard work. The balance he maintained between his work life and personal life was remarkable. No one ever worked harder than Winston Churchill. He also was remarkable in his tenacity. He would simply never allow any problems, mistakes, national disasters, or even war to get him down. Criticism never got him down either. His power of physical and mental recuperation was astounding. Most importantly, and something that has resonated with me for decades, was Churchill's absence of hatred. As tough a warrior and leader as he was, he could, nevertheless, light up a room with his smile, humor, and mere presence. His heart was joyful, regardless of the evil that surrounded him. He was always able to deal with the negative, not dwell on it, and move on to his next challenge. I doubt there will be another inspirational figure like Winston Churchill in my lifetime, though there is always hope.

Over the years, among the most important lessons I have learned for becoming an effective leader and mentor to my employees is the high value of confronting problems by making sure, I, as the leader, have the proper attitude and approach toward interacting with them. By that I mean trying very hard to find the "good" in people first, if at all possible, and it usually is. To see their good and worthy personal attributes first, explore who they are as individuals, and essentially find out what makes them tick. This is what I call *purposeful problem solving.*

This is especially important when you are dealing with an employee or teammate on an issue that arises or a problem that requires a higher degree of problem solving. Once a relationship based on respect, trust, and goodwill has been established, it is then so much easier to move on to a good discussion about the problem that needs addressing.

John Maxwell calls it the one hundred point 1 percent principle, which basically says that leaders should find the 1 percent in a person that they can truly affirm, and then give it 100 percent of their attention. I have found Maxwell's theory to be practical and effective, especially when confronting problems in the workplace.

For example, it is very easy for a leader to address a problem with a long verbal criticism, if not a full-blown verbal attack, that can easily come across as demeaning. That is the old way of management that was followed by so many leaders for decades, as well as just basic human nature. I have found that is not a very productive way to work with folks and gain their full commitment to problem solving, especially when dealing with Gen X'ers and Millennials. When people feel threatened or berated, they often stop listening. Once they tune you out, they often become defensive and work very hard to prepare their response to the perceived threat, rather than fully listening and appreciating the need to resolve the real problem at hand. When that happens, little is achieved on a constructive basis, and more damage is done to the employer/employee relationship than the actual act of solving the problem.

It too often sets in motion what I call blame dodging or blame spreading rather than real meaningful problem solving. It also greatly increases the odds that an otherwise good employee may begin to feel unappreciated, leading to the possible loss of that employee either through lack of motivation or his or her decision to terminate the employment. And through all of this, the problem never actually does get solved and can in large part remain while the otherwise good employee is gone!

And, in my opinion, *words really do matter!* What we all say and do in the workplace, just as at home, has a direct impact on others—both positively and negatively. I have tried to incorporate what I have learned about the power of positive communication into how I manage my employees each and every day of my life. I am reminded of a quote by C. S. Lewis. He says about the power of words: "Don't use words too big for the subject. Don't say infinitely when you mean very; otherwise you'll have no word left when you want to talk about something really infinite."

While it is inevitable that we as leaders must always confront important issues in the workplace, it is also critically important that we do so with the right approach—with the *right words*. And, when searching for just the right words to say in any business situation, offering them with a spirit of *care and consideration* can often more fully engage someone to enthusiastically tackle a problem. It will also motivate folks to embrace that *team spirit* and motivate them to become active participants in being part of the solution. I have seen firsthand what happens when people don't feel demeaned, blamed, or attacked, but, rather, feel an appreciation for the manner in which their leader worked to solve the problem. Ultimately, they are happier and more productive team members. *Caring communication* also encourages an environment where everyone is motivated to make positive decisions, not only for one single issue on any given day, but rather for the long haul, where problems are inevitable in the life cycle of any business.

In addition to being an effective problem solver by approaching problems in a positive and caring way, effective leaders know the value of *mentoring* and *coaching* their employees, desk mates, and teammates. Ironically, this leadership tenet was expressed so well by the University of Tennessee football running back Alvin Kamara, who said after a particularly devastating loss for the team in 2015: "Keep everybody going. Everybody has to keep their heads up, and keep grinding. We talk about it every day, and we have each other's backs. That's the motto going into this week. I got your back, Coach Jones's got everybody's backs, we got the coach's back, and we are just going to keep working."

While that very disappointing loss could have divided the team and caused them to go into a major downward cycle of more losses, the Volunteer football team instead pulled together and followed that loss by winning the next six games to finish the season strong. Ultimately, head coach Butch Jones did not rant and rave after the disappointing loss, or call out any particular players. Instead he chose to continue his team approach of encouraging players to have each other's backs and to stay together as a team. Only by staying positive and taking a team-first approach was coach Jones able to save the season and actually turn it around into one that finished strong.

The same team spirit was echoed by Peyton Manning, the Denver Broncos quarterback and fourteen-year NFL veteran. He believes that respect for others is a hallmark of effective leadership. Here's what he said: "You can't lead unless you have learned and earned respect." He was well aware that even though he was in the NFL for many years before joining the Broncos, he still went to the weight room early every day, was the first person to show up at practice, and the last one to leave. His goal: to earn the *respect* of his teammates. And it was thrilling to see Peyton and the Broncos end the 2015–16 football season by winning none other than Super Bowl Fifty!

It also really helps lead to the building of a strong bench, so to speak, meaning the growth of current employees into future leaders in the company. We at Churchill Mortgage believe that the bottom line of management success is to work hard at teaching, coaching, and mentoring our employees so that they develop into highly contributing members of our team. By doing that, we grow as a group, as a cohesive team, and achieve much higher levels of business success than we otherwise would just wishing and hoping everyone does their job well. Further, we have institutionalized what Dave Ramsey daily tells America about Churchill Mortgage, namely that we have the *heart of a teacher*.

In a recent e-mail I read, I came across some interesting thoughts penned by Oaktree Capital's CEO, Howard Marks, where he reiterated his long-held opinion that, "In order to be successful, an investor has to understand not just finance, accounting, and economics, but also psychology." He makes an excellent and insightful point.

Being in many respects a teacher, and having the heart of a teacher, has always been a core conviction of mine. I no doubt inherited this mind-set from my pastor/teacher father. It is just as important in building a solid, productive, and happy workplace as it is at home, in the classroom, or building a great church. Many of the business gurus I have studied—such as John Maxwell, Todd Duncan, Cecil Kemp, Michael Burt, and others who have come to Churchill to impart their wisdom to our employees nationwide, have stressed the importance of giving the gift of *mentorship,* as well as imparting the *core foundations* that have proven to be crucial to a business's success or failure while incorporating a faith-based and purpose-driven foundation. For us, those core foundations of honesty, humility, integrity, teacher, attitude, stewardship, philanthropy, life-long learning, balance, and broomsweeper have served as the cornerstone for our employees and helped build a corporate culture based on those key tenets. But, ultimately, they took me many years to perfect and implement, and they would be merely hollow words if I didn't practice what I preach. So, to be judged on my actions rather than intentions, I've spent nearly thirty years walking the walk, so to speak, and found that certain positive behaviors that I've found not only work for me, but for anyone who wants to live a happy, productive, and healthy life.

One could say it is my personal Ten Commandments; I like to call them my *daily disciplines.*

The ultimate goal for me and our management team is to develop and then utilize these daily disciplines as a key part of becoming successful in business and in life. I have purposely taught my children and many employees over the years what I believe to be a very high-value idea or strategy, and that is, to be a disciplined and patient person by consistently applying core principles into daily life. What are those core principles and daily disciplines that have worked for me? Here are a few that have impacted my life and the lives of my employees both in the workplace and in life generally.

1. The first is to just get up and get going! It is too easy to be jolted awake by the alarm clock and then hit the snooze button, not once but two or three times. I have learned that the first five-to-seven minutes of actually getting up are never easy, but the day starts out better by not procrastinating. To jumpstart the morning, I also believe in drinking six to eight ounces of water. Our bodies become a little dehydrated as we sleep at night, and by just drinking water early in the morning it makes folks feel better and more energetic.

I actually began to do this regularly after a doctor friend of mine gave me these words of wisdom more than thirty years ago: "Shower to cleanse our inner bodies, just as we take a shower to cleanse our outer bodies each day."

2. Setting aside a few minutes for time to reflect on the things that positively impact our lives and cause us to be thankful to God should be a priority! I usually spend a few minutes every day doing a short devotion as a way to get my day off to a productive start. I ask God to "provide me the physical and mental strength for the inevitable issues that will confront me during the day." The Trappist monk Thomas Merton once said, "No man is an island;" I can attest that I need all the help I can receive on a regular basis, especially from the creator of the universe!

3. Whether one is preparing for the workday at the office or at home, spending ten to fifteen minutes thinking about what is most important to get accomplished is critical for realizing and achieving goals. It is so very easy to get sidetracked by things that are not really important, but that is simply not an option. The notion was reinforced by a short pamphlet I read many years ago called *The Tyranny of the Urgent*. It helped me to really begin to focus much more of my energy on the critical things I needed to get done, knowing that the remaining noncritical items would eventually get done or simply just go away.

4. There is no doubt that exercise plays a huge role in mental and physical alertness, stamina, and overall good health. Now I am not saying everyone has to hit the gym every day for two hours, and, frankly, I have never been one to do that. However, it is very important to have some level of reasonable daily exercise, if for no other reason than to be able to accomplish your hopes and dreams. It is important to feel good, to have physical stamina, and there is no legitimate way to do that over a lifetime if folks don't pay attention to their personal health at some basic level. I've encouraged my employees to take control of their daily health by: taking a ten-to-twenty minute walk,

parking several aisles out in the parking lot and walking a little farther into and out of the office, taking the stairs rather than the elevator, and getting in a little exercise throughout the day.

5. Maintaining a reasonable weight is good for the body as well as for the soul. It helps all of us feel better about ourselves and gives us the ability to work hard and not feel overwhelmed. For me, I have found that by simply weighing myself every morning, I have been able to keep my weight under control. I am not fanatical about weight in general, but I have found that staying within a reasonable range helps me feel better and keeps my daily exercise routine on track.

6. And, of course, there is no greater feeling of satisfaction than by helping someone else. All of our employees know to be proactive in looking for someone that truly needs help, and then be that person to make a difference. It's the small things that can have the greatest impact, such as providing someone with food that otherwise might be hungry; helping someone that is close to being evicted from a home or apartment by providing him or her the financial resources that are desperately needed; or reaching out to someone that is in real despair over a personal situation and being the one to just be there and listen. There are so many people who are truly in need, and doing these acts of kindness can truly changes lives for the better. Additionally, anyone who gives back in these simple ways will be amazed at how much better he or she will feel about himself or herself, which is the surprising by-product of personal philanthropy.

7. To read and learn each and every day is a must! Why is it that we attend school for at least thirteen years from the time we start kindergarten through high school, then move on to college for another four years, then graduate school, and still think that our learning years are finished? The older and more experienced I have become in my business and personal life, I realize how much more there is to learn! I remember watching my dad sitting in the den reading books late into the night long after my mom, Steve, and I

went to bed. Dad instilled in me the love of reading. To this day I spend at least two hours every day reading business books and other books and periodicals, both in print and in digital format, focusing on religion, politics, and sports, as well as wonderful novels by some of my favorite authors, such as Brad Thor and Tom Clancy.

8. Chill, sleep, and relax! It has been recommended by countless doctors and health specialists over many, many years the high value of rest, and, likewise, it has been documented that folks also can get too much sleep, which can be equally bad for one's health. I have found that getting about six or seven hours of good sleep each night works best for me. I do that by turning off the lights and television, sleeping in a dark, quiet, and cool room, and just letting go of the day.

9. Most important for me, and what I try to instill in my employees, is to connect with family. There is no greater joy than to spend time with a loved one, and as I have now found even more so, grandkids. There is a very good reason why they are referred to as grandkids, by the way; it's because they are absolutely grand! I have felt that familial connection throughout my life, and it has made all the difference. There were many wonderful times when I received that daily call from my mother when she would typically say, "What are you doing, Son." She wasn't calling me generally with anything critically important but rather just to hear my voice and make sure everything was all right. She loved just checking in, and I have found how much I like doing that now with my own children and grandchildren. Most of the time my daily calls to my sweet wife, children and grandchildren, my brother or my father, typically last no more than a few minutes, and yet when I don't connect with them for more than a couple of days at a time, I feel as if I am missing out on one of life's most important treasures.

There are additional daily disciplines to weave into the business day, which I have mentioned in other chapters of *Keep Chopping Wood*. Most important, though, is to really determine what are the nonnegotiables. What are those things that bring the highest value in the business day that simply need to be done? What are those activities that could really drive people to much higher levels of success if they only devoted more of their time and energy toward achieving them? In an earlier chapter, I discussed the "40-10-5-2 rule" and how the numbers really matter. If I was a betting man, I would wager a lot of money that the numbers in most people's businesses are not dramatically different than the "40-10-5-2" numbers I referenced, no matter in which business a person is involved. It is so important to know those specific numbers and then make a commitment to do daily the high-value activities that will drive a person to those numbers. Being persistently consistent in doing the right activities with the right business partner over time is an extremely worthwhile endeavor.

It seems that many folks I've come across in business, especially some in the financial world, haven't seen the value in doing many of these things on a consistent basis. Rather, they choose to move through life in a more random and happenstance fashion, enjoying whatever seems to be easy and fun for the day with little thought or real concern for tomorrow. It seems that they believe activity equates to success, without much regard for the quality of those activities! I believe that the most truly meaningful and impactful success does not come overnight but, rather, from years and years of investing one's time in the right activities. Benjamin Graham, author of *The Intelligent Investor*, so wisely said, "By developing your discipline and courage, you can refuse to let other people's mood swings govern your financial destiny. In the end, how your investments behave is much less important than how you behave."

Another *right activity* is realizing that we should live our lives with thought, grace, and gusto, which many might think would be counterintuitive. Our employees know that they are free to be creative and experimental as long as they carefully weigh their decision making and communicate thoughtfully and respectfully with others. I hope we all would say to ourselves when we take stock of our lives, "I'm glad I did," and not end up saying, "I wish I had!"

For example, how many of us have made New Year's resolutions to work out more or lose weight; however, near the end of the year, we often have to say to ourselves, "I wish I had!" Too often we see folks who are close to their retirement age but are not able to retire anywhere near where they had hoped because of not paying attention to their financial situations earlier in their lives. Too often and, sadly, too late, they say, "I wish I had" instead of being able to say, "I'm glad I did!" Others spend too much time working to earn money and have a great career and not enough time investing in their children, and when they near the end of their lives, they too, may say, "I wish I had" instead of saying, "I'm glad I did!"

I have tried in my business and personal life to live by those precious words "I'm glad I did," which brings me back to why I finally made the decision to write this book.

About one year ago, Lawson came into my office, sat on the ledge of the window facing out to our parking lot and asked me a question. This happens frequently, so I just expected him to ask me a technical question about a mortgage calculation or a business question about how to improve our customer service or bottom line. Instead, he said to me, "Dad, I've learned so much from you, and I know all of our employees feel the same way. I know that for a fact because of so many conversations I've had with our employees about what you've done to help other people." Of course, I was humbled to hear Lawson say that, but I knew he knew that this is just part of our collective DNA, and it was really no big deal. "Dad, I wanted to tell you about a conversation I had with Stephanie. She told me about the time you secretly paid for that woman to get a new set of teeth. Wow, Dad, that was awesome! You've had so many experiences like this, and I've been talking to Matt, Megan, and Shayna, and we think you should write a book. You've been an inspiration to so many people all around the country, and we think you should go for it."

Lawson finally gave me the impetus to put my life's experiences in a book format, offering them as a gift, wrapped in paper with gratitude, deference, and love—to give folks a glimpse into a life that has hopefully been well-lived, one filled with triumphs, heartbreaks, and redemption. As a preacher's son, my aim is not to preach, but to help folks understand and appreciate what I have learned over my lifetime and consider how those life lessons might apply to their everyday lives. To offer emotional courage, to never say, "You should do this," but, rather, consider all the options in making the big decisions that come along as part of all of our glorious and precious lives. To give encouragement in times of trouble, faith when hope may be lost, and the power and confidence to know that positive change can and will happen, and to just keep chopping wood.

Finally, I hope folks will know that my ultimate goal in life is simply to be remembered as a good man, a good man to my family, a good man to my employees and, most of all, a good man in the eyes of God.

Epilogue

Well, I want to say thank you for investing your valuable time to read my book. I hope you have been inspired, and maybe even motivated to incorporate some of the ideas I have shared about real and lasting success. As you know by now, I believe strongly that real success has to be something that brings more than financial rewards. It has to also provide a sense of contentment, peace, and joy. I want to leave you with a couple of additional thoughts that have done me well personally, on both a business and personal level.

My longtime good friend, author, and businessman Cecil Kemp says if a company wants to have a culture of excellence, then its leaders must define that, they must actually live it out, and they must lead their followers to practice it on an ongoing basis. When a leader practices leading more as a super servant than desiring to be perceived as a superstar, then he or she fosters an environment that over time breeds excellence. While I have never built or led a company with tens of thousands of employees, I have had the good fortune to found and lead companies with hundreds of employees, and in each instance I have attempted to create a family culture. By that I simply mean creating an environment where all employees treat each other as family. When I think of family, I think of my wife, parents and grandparents, my children, and my aunts and uncles. While we all have our disagreements and at times have strong arguments, we still so highly value each other that we would stand up and fight for each other in almost any situation. While I certainly love and value my friendships, there is still not the same level of involvement that I have for a family member. I would dare to say that is usually the same for most other folks.

Cecil further coaches that common goals, values, harmony, unity, cooperation, care, and respect for one another are tangible things that showcase what a family culture entails. Many of my other business coaches and mentors echo this tenet as well. Valuing each person relatively equally, and looking out for the good of all, helps enlist all team members in developing a lasting culture of excellence and accountability to one another. Leaders who desire this type of company culture do not pit one team member against another. When one wins at the expense of another, then the result usually fosters a me-first mentality, and the net gain for the company is at best minimal, and can be extremely costly. It has been said that when an employee exits a company, it is typically because he or she is not happy with the leader. The cost to replace that person is roughly equal to ten months of that person's salary plus the cost of the new employee's salary, which is usually more than the departing person's salary. The numbers too often simply don't add up.

More than just the bottom line, getting an employee to do what is best for the entire team should be a prime goal of any great leader. The focus should always be on what is best for the organization without concern for who gets the credit. The welfare of an individual employee is to some extent intertwined with the welfare of all employees. When we view each other more like brothers and sisters than just employees, we tend to really care more, go the extra mile, and cheer each other on toward success. The whole is greater than the sum of its parts, so to say. I have seen firsthand over many years in business that truly great accomplishments can be realized when we all really care about each other and work together to build toward the greater goal.

My father taught me in my early adult years that "Everything rises or falls based on leadership! Families, churches, businesses, nonprofits, universities, governments, and any type of organization basically can only go as far as the leader is capable of taking it. A strong leader with vision and the ability to articulate that vision can inspire followers to accomplish much more than a weak leader who might lead more from fear and has little ability to articulate whatever vision he or she might have."

As you have read in *Keep Chopping Wood*, you know that I believe any success I have been able to enjoy over the years has come from the goodness of an almighty God who created us, and loves us so deeply. The Word of God teaches us that He knew us by our name *before* He laid the foundations of the world (Jeremiah 1:5, Ephesians 1:4, Romans 8:29). That is powerful stuff! The guy who actually created the world and everything in it knew me as Mike before He went to work on this place!

Further, the Bible teaches us that He takes notice when a little sparrow falls from a tree (Matthew 10:29). Now think about that for a moment. How many millions or possibly even billions of sparrows are there in this vast world? Yet, God takes note when any one of them falls. To me, that is a completely awesome thought. Further, the Bible tells us that He even knows the number of hairs on our head (Matthew 10:30).

What I am trying to say is that there is a wonderful and loving God who knows each of us, and He knows us well. He created each and every one of us, He knows us by our name, and He cares for us more than we can possibly know. I take great comfort in that truth. While this life can and does throw curveballs at each of us at various points in our lives and which sometimes bring us to our knees, we can know with confidence that God is there to help us. An old song has a line that says, "He never sleeps; He never slumbers. He watches over us both night and day." We can have a high level of peace and contentment in our lives, whether rich or poor, famous or unknown to most of the world, knowing that He really does care for us. Matthew 10:31 teaches us that He loves us more than the sparrows, and we now know how He is so aware of their plight. If we simply acknowledge that God is real, that He is there, and we trust our lives to Him, no matter how many times we mess up and fail, we can rest assured in the knowledge that He will bring about His will for each of us individually, as we are His family. Jeremiah 29:11 says, "For I know the plans I have for you," declares the LORD, "plans to prosper you and not to harm you, plans to give you hope and a future." I know of nothing that provides me more confidence, peace, and contentment in my life than that knowledge. And for those of different faiths, believing in something greater than yourself should give life much greater meaning, satisfaction, comfort, and fulfillment.

I love an old song, which for the life of me I can't remember, that has a great line that says something like this: "I've read the back of the book, and we win!" What does that "win" look like? I believe in a literal Heaven, and I believe that despite all my failures, which have been many, that someday I will actually see that Heaven. I will be able to see my precious mother once again together with my grandparents and so many other folks who have meant so much to me that have now passed.

Some might say that is just pie in the sky, and that is all right. I have no problem with anyone who sees these things differently from me. My sense of self and my personal confidence is not tied up in whether others agree with me on this point. I love and respect so many people who see this differently than I do, and it might just be that I am able to do that because of God's love and grace. I certainly would have not understood that on my own.

I am reminded of an old saying my father told me many time times that went something like this: "If there is no God, then nothing really matters, but, if there is a God, then nothing else really matters."

Matt Clarke recently reminded me of a biblical scripture in the Old Testament book of I Kings 3:9 where King Solomon asked God for an understanding heart so that he could lead his people well and be able to discern right from wrong. That is a great reminder for us as leaders to truly have that type of heart. Having an understanding heart is not a weakness but, to me, a great strength. Because having a sincere desire to lead well, knowing that God provides us wisdom, we will indeed do just that. In fact, James 1:5 instructs us to ask God for wisdom, and it further tells us that if we will, then He will give it to us generously! The best leaders—whether they be in business, politics, medicine, or any field—deeply understand at some level that when the heart is put on the back shelf, leadership is in jeopardy.

My deepest hope and prayer is that as you have taken your valuable time to read my book, it has in some small way inspired you to consider what God wants in your own life. He can make a difference whether you are a CEO, just starting out in business, or if you are a parent, student, or anyone who wants to have a meaningful and fulfilling life. While I cannot promise you a life without problems, I can promise you that your life will have a superstar major-league-level player on your side! He has been the major difference maker in the lives of me and my family without question.

Mike Hardwick has *kept chopping wood* for most of his life. His belief that by never giving up, never quitting, and striving to be a better person, not a bitter person, is the prescription for a happy life. While seeking "progress, not perfection," and knowing the satisfaction of putting in a hard-day's work, he has achieved the goals he has set for his life. He hopes you will also do the same by striving to *keep chopping wood*.

About the Authors

Lawson H. (Mike) Hardwick

Lawson H. (Mike) Hardwick III is founder and president of Brentwood, Tennessee-based Churchill Mortgage Corporation, a leader in the mortgage industry providing conventional, FHA, VA, and USDA residential mortgages across thirty-three states and the District of Columbia. With more than thirty-five years of mortgage and banking experience, Hardwick is a highly successful mortgage lender and a seasoned businessman. With experience as a mortgage, insurance, and real estate broker, the span of knowledge and expertise Hardwick possesses is invaluable. Focused on providing a top-quality experience to consumers, Hardwick has proven himself as a successful entrepreneur, building and maintaining multiple financial companies.

The first half of Hardwick's career was spent in commercial and investment banking with two nationally known firms. In the early 1980s, he founded a condo conversion company, which grew to be the third-largest in the nation. Shortly after the peak of that business, Hardwick became one of the principal founders of Franklin National Bank in Franklin, Tennessee. He served as an executive vice president until 1992, and then founded Churchill Mortgage. He continued serving on the Board of Directors for Franklin National Bank for several years thereafter. The bank was later acquired by Fifth Third Bank.

Hardwick graduated from Gateway College in St. Louis, Missouri, where he received a bachelor's degree in theology and music. He received a BBA in finance from Belmont University in Nashville, Tennessee, where he was a member of the university's baseball team. Hardwick has served on many boards and committees, including Friends of the Arts Board at Belmont University and the Finance & Endowment Committee for Christ Church Nashville. He is also a founder and board member of Real Estate Services of America, Escrow Services of Tennessee, Churchill Agency, and Equity Express.

A life-long resident of Nashville, Hardwick resides there with his wife, Stephanie, and is a proud father of two daughters and two sons.

Dava Guerin

Dava Guerin is the author of *Unbreakable Bonds: The Mighty Moms and Wounded Warriors of Walter Reed*. It was released to critical acclaim on November 4, 2014, and is published by Skyhorse Publishing. She is also the coauthor of *Presidents, Kings and Convicts*, the political memoir of former member of Congress Bob Clement (D-TN). Guerin is also a freelance writer with more than forty stories published in regional and national periodicals, newspapers, and social media outlets. She was also founder and president of Guerin Public Relations Inc., where she managed major communications programs for Fortune 100 companies, as well as government agencies, political figures, and nonprofit organizations. She has extensive media relations and experience, having worked on major national and international events including: the Bicentennial of the US Constitution, Live8, the 2000 Republican National Convention, the Liberty Medal, Welcome America, Mrs. Bush's Story Time, the President's Summit for America's Future, and many others. She also has managed dignitary appearances for major celebrities, US presidents and world leaders, and also serves as communications director for the US Association of Former Members of Congress.

She holds a bachelor of arts degree in English and literature from Goddard College and a master's degree in organizational behavior from Temple University, where she graduated summa cum laude. She also spent a summer abroad attending the University of London. She volunteers her time helping wounded warriors and their families. She resides in Berlin, Maryland, with her husband, Terry.